ADOLESCENCE
AND POVERTY

ADOLESCENCE AND POVERTY

Challenge for the 1990s

Peter B. Edelman & Joyce Ladner
Editors

CENTER FOR NATIONAL POLICY PRESS
WASHINGTON, D.C.

Copyright © 1991 by
Center for National Policy Press

Distributed by arrangement with
University Press of America, Inc.
4720 Boston Way
Lanham, MD 20706

European Distribution by
Eurospan
3 Henrietta Street
London WC2E 8LU England

Library of Congress Cataloging-in-Publication Data

Adolescence and poverty : challenge for the 1990s
/ Peter B. Edelman & Joyce Ladner, editors.
p.   cm.
1. Poor teenagers—United States.
2. Minority teenagers—United States.
3. Teenagers—Government policy—United States.
I. Edelman, Peter B.   II. Ladner, Joyce A.
HQ796.A3323   1991   305.23'5—dc20   91-16446 CIP

ISBN 0–944237–31–2 (alk. paper)
ISBN 0–944237–32–0 (pbk. : alk. paper)

All Center for National Policy Press books are produced on acid-free paper
which exceeds the minimum standards set by the National Historical
Publication and Records Commission

CONTENTS

INTRODUCTION

Peter B. Edelman and Joyce Ladner

ADOLESCENCE, ALWAYS A PERILOUS passage, has become for literally millions of American young people a voyage that never reaches the other shore.

Most American youth can expect to navigate the transition to a career, family responsibility, and other adult roles without lasting damage from the rebellion, the questioning, and the dislocation that are typical of the adolescent period (although any parent of an adolescent will express grave uncertainty as whether it will all work out).

Adolescence is not a simple time even for the minority who will be fortunate enough to obtain a four-year college degree. It is more difficult for those who stop after two years of post-secondary education, and it is more difficult by far for those who do not attend college at all.

But for a large proportion of the troublingly large numbers who grow up in poverty today, especially if they are members of historically disadvantaged racial or ethnic minorities, the journey has become mission impossible—resulting in problems and outcomes so devastating that recovery into an adulthood of self-sufficiency and marriage, let alone any broader societal participation, is out of the question.

For American children in general, growing up is an infinitely more complicated task than the one that current adults confronted in the past.

Community institutions and neighborhood ties have weakened in city, suburb, and rural America alike. Many more children are growing up in a culture of disengagement, lacking either close enough relationships with parents who are both working long hours outside the home in order to make ends meet (or with a parent who is absent due to divorce) or sufficient positive socializing opportunities with

1

other adults in the community to make up for the gaps at home. Especially in recent years, America has suffered from a leadership vacuum in terms of positive adult role models, societally as well as politically.

Economically, too many young people are confronted with only two choices in terms of work: a limited number of professional, often high technology possibilities, or a world of relatively low-income service jobs—McDonalds, the proverbial "Mickey Ds," is the metaphor. The blue collar positions that were the avenue to the suburbs for millions of Americans after World War II have shrunk precipitously.

If adolescence is more difficult for many than in the past, it has become a minefield for the poor, especially poor minorities, and even more especially for those who live in the inner-city areas of concentrated poverty. There, drugs and gangs have created a level of violence and destruction of lives—instantaneous death by AK-47 and death-in-life by a pattern of injection—that is unprecedented in modern American history. Babies in their cribs are killed by stray bullets and pre-teenage children are impressed or inveigled into gangs and the drug industry, as employees or users or both. Many are the children from strong albeit economically struggling families who fall prey to the hazards of the streets.

Stereotypically, the problems of poor youth, particularly those in the inner-city, are regarded as problems of race. In many if not most people's minds, the term "underclass" is a code word for black ghetto residents. There is a serious racial element to poverty, which should not be denied and must inform policy, but the importance of class in the equation should not be understated. Upper- and middle-class children who manifest serious behavior problems see a psychiatrist or get labels of handicapped or developmentally disabled and are sent to special schools paid for through programs like the Education of All Handicapped Children Act. Poor children are labelled neglected, removed from their parents, and placed in foster care. When they get older, their behavior makes them clients of the juvenile justice system. The rich send their problem children (sons, anyway) to military school; the children of the poor are sent to reform school.

Adolescents with problems, especially minorities, have never been attractive objects of public policy. They are not cute and cuddly like three year olds and, even with the best of efforts, success rates are not as high as those that come from broad prevention programs focused on infants and small children.

The fallacy in concentrating on small children, of course, is that prevention geared to early childhood doesn't prevent everything.

There is always and inevitably a clientele for intervention at a later age. The irony, as the essays in this volume will show, is that adolescence is in fact a developmental period rather analogous to early childhood, in which young people are open to change and are indeed changing rapidly. It is a time when well-designed public policy initiatives have more promise than has been popularly supposed. And it is a time when intervention is emphatically still preventive in relation to the adulthood to follow, even though the young person may already have manifested problems which it is the purpose of the intervention to address.

Even in the 1960s when, as the mythology now has it, we were throwing money at problems, we did relatively poorly in the way of public programs to address the problems of low-income adolescents. The Job Corps was evaluated a success, but it was expensive and reached relatively few people. The federal summer jobs program has continued as a kind of permanent band-aid to maintain calm in the streets on hot nights, but there never was a serious, funded, persevering year-round effort for out-of-school out-of-work youth. President Jimmy Carter had a task force on the subject which proposed a serious piece of legislation that he sent up to Congress, but the bill did not become law, and even if it had, it would not have survived the Reagan onslaught on federal domestic programs.

The problem was never invisible. Claude Brown's chronicle of widespread heroin addiction in Harlem, *Manchild in the Promised Land*, was read by a generation of policymakers. The riots of Watts, Newark, Detroit, and dozens of other places brought the problem of inner-city poverty and its effects into America's living rooms. Even rural poverty—harder to see, but also pervasive—had its days and months in the news in the 1960s.

Nonetheless, from the election of Richard Nixon on, the nation's policy was to look the other way. Money was spent on the poor in the indexing of Social Security, the enactment of the Supplemental Security Income program for the elderly and disabled, the vast expansion of food stamps, and the maturing of Medicaid, but no special effort was made to enable poor young people to become self-sufficient.

With the first oil shock of 1973, the game was not only completely up, but, as Andrew Sum and W. Neal Fogg demonstrate in their chapter in this volume, a long-term decline in the fortunes of young workers began, unmet by any constructive public policy response. This trend has been a disaster for young men in particular, and even worse, for poor minority youth of both sexes.

So we have failed an entire generation. The inner-city streets, never a safe place, have become a vicious whirlpool, sucking ever-increasing numbers of young people into crime, violence, drugs, and unduly early parenting. Rural poverty has increased especially among the young. In the eighties we learned, and properly so, to talk of the individual responsibility that people must take for themselves, but we also forgot, quite unacceptably, to understand that those young people whose lives are being wasted so horribly did not get that way by themselves. They are a product of our society, and we bear a measure of responsibility for that.

The purpose of this volume is to describe the current situation—to map the minefield that life has become for the poor and especially for low-income minority youth, and to make some suggestions for how the minefield might be traversed. There are strategies for survival here, and insights policymakers should have as they design policy for the future.

We write with great humility. We know the complexity of the problems we are addressing. We have no simple or sure-fire solutions to offer. We share responsibility for the tragedy that is intensifying each and every day in our streets. We have no illusion that our warnings or the analysis we have gathered here will be the things that jolt our nation into action. If we were all that brilliant, we would have precise, guaranteed policies to offer, and we would have offered them a long time ago.

There are some key points to stress.

One, adolescents are people undergoing rapid change. They are not in a fixed and immutable state. There are policies that will make a difference.

Two, the idea of community should be a key element of policy. An important aim should be the building of community everywhere—nowhere more important than in the chaos of the inner city. This is no easy task, but an essential one because solutions solely directed at individuals miss the influence of the environment around them.

Three, the idea of community also means that the larger community should take responsibility for developing the solutions and helping to carry them out: not government alone, but everyone in the local community—all the civic leadership, business, labor, educators, churches, foundations, and the people. In post-World War II America in particular, the idea of community—of the responsibility of each of us for all of us—was lost in the headlong rush to the suburbs and the misguided belief nurtured by the postwar economic boom that all of us could make it on our own without any help from others and those who didn't had only themselves to blame. This was wrong even then, as government policy sent millions of people to college on the G.I.

Bill and helped even larger numbers to purchase the homes they had dreamed of owning.

This leads to four. A major lesson of the past thirty years must be that government cannot do the whole job but that it must play a role. If the naive faith of the sixties was that government would do the whole job and the rest of us could sit back and do nothing, the myth of the eighties was that government had no role to play at all. The synthesis for the nineties must be that all of us, government included, have a role.

Five, there are no magic bullets. If the sixties featured the simplistic view that a miracle cure would be found for poverty and the eighties stood for the opposite view that nothing works in that regard, the nineties must be the time when we agree that simultaneous effort along many fronts is needed in terms of education, economic opportunity, safety in the streets, creation of role models, and more.

Six, money is not the only answer, but it is part of the answer. We have to deal with structural problems in failing schools and rigid bureaucracies, but we must also understand that there is no way of doing the job on the cheap.

Seven, enabling self-sufficiency is the name of the game more than any other single aim. Young men and women who are self-supporting will not be public assistance recipients. They will be more likely to get married and they will be better parents. A major design aim of policies should be that they will have a positive effect in promoting self-sufficiency.

Eight, the point of entry into adulthood—the time when families form or do not form—is a key leverage point. We know, for example, that one key predictor of a child's success is whether his or her mother has finished high school. Interventions to get young mothers to finish high school will therefore not only contribute to their own self-sufficiency but also to their children's future. Similarly, since so many young children who are targets of policies like Head Start have parents who are themselves just entering adulthood, there will be far more promise in the interventions on behalf of the children if there are simultaneous interventions to assist the parents.

Nine, the schools are a significant forum for policy initiatives. In addition to overall school reform as an agenda, there are promising steps for at-risk youth which should be undertaken. These involve an appreciation of the fact that mentoring and role model relationships are extremely important, and the fact that summer learning has a demonstrated effect in preventing at-risk youth from losing too much of last year's academic accomplishment over the summer. Schools should consider identifying students at risk as early as the sixth grade, and connecting them with mentors and getting them into a summer learning experience. When the student is old enough to work, the summer jobs program should be modified so that the student can learn and work on a combined basis during the summer.

Ten, more communities should explore combinations of the Boston Compact and I Have a Dream programs, to guarantee entry level jobs and college, as appropriate, to those who stay in school and graduate from inner-city high schools. There has now been enough experience under these programs to merit federal support in an appropriate way.

Eleven, we cannot afford not to act. Over 80 percent of the new young workers entering the labor force during this decade will be people who are not native-born white males. In other words, they will be either female, African-American or other racial minorities born in this country, or people born outside this country. And we need all of them, because this is the period when the products of the "baby bust" are coming along. We are experiencing an overall diminution in the number of people even potentially available to enter the labor force. We need everyone's productivity.

We might say a brief word about the essays in this volume. They cover the basic interactions of adolescence and poverty from both theoretical and anecdotal perspectives. They discuss the critical issues of education and employment, and they offer separate assessments of the difficulties facing girls and boys in being poor and going through adolescence.

There are specifics about which they appear to disagree, such as on the value of the jobs some high school students currently are getting; on the exact impact of school-based discriminatory attitudes toward racial minority students; or, on how the relative damage caused by inadequate parenting falls as between disadvantaged girls and disadvantaged boys. These—though interesting differences and worth further research—do not detract significantly from the general consistency of fact and analysis found in the chapters.

Robert Coles begins the volume with a characteristically eloquent contrast between the worries and concerns of a white upper middle class child and a black child of modest income. The portrait emerges through Coles' sensitive interviewing process, as always, and it sets the stage for the remainder of the volume. Coles introduces us to "the way class and race give shape to a family's sense of what is possible, [and] what is impossible," and he reminds us that the world of one's own parents and neighborhood "is more significant in the psychological and moral development of children than has often been acknowledged by some of us social scientists and physicians."

Laurence Steinberg's essay places the experiences of poor youth in the context of "the logic of adolescence" generally, to use his term. He tells us that the developmental agenda of adolescence is to prepare for the intimacy of emotional interpersonal relationships ("love"), the taking of personal responsibility ("work"), and the assumption of social responsibiity ("citizenship"). He characterizes the central feature of adolescence as "adolescent egocentrism" (all parents of adolescents will understand this well), which he says includes extreme self-consciousness about how one is viewed by one's peers, and a sense of personal uniqueness—a belief that one is simply not at the same risk of harm as anyone else.

Steinberg argues that too many adolescents today lack a close relationship with a non-familial adult, and experience a sense of "rolelessness" as a consequence. He charges the adult community with taking the responsibility to offer guidance that will reduce the number of youth "whose adolescent experience is characterized by excessive autonomy, rolelessness, and risk."

Andrew Sum and W. Neal Fogg give an important statistical overview, presenting among other things a series of unemployment, labor market participation, and earnings figures that show structural shifts and weakness in the economy which first appeared in the early 1970s. These developments have had the worst effects on young workers, and particularly racial minorities and the poor. The impacts have been most severe on those with the least educational attainment, with even the previously critical high school diploma having lost a lot of its value. As a result, the disparities between the poor and everyone else have been growing steadily since 1973. The Sum and Fogg paper presents a devastating picture of the earnings experience of young minorities since 1973, which has reversed a strong upward trend that had been operative since 1959. It would appear on the basis of these statistics that the deterioration in the statistics on marriage and family formation among young minority people since the early 1970s is no accident, but rather is directly connected to the spectacular economic deterioration that has occurred.

The focus of Judith Musick's essay is on young women. She describes how experiences typically associated with poverty and disadvantage disrupt the adolescent developmental process and lead to premature adulthood and unfulfilled potential. She tells us that key developmental purposes are served when a girl from a damaged low-income family engages in early sexual activity and parenthood, and challenges those who would intervene programmatically to mesh developmental readiness with realistic opportunities to succeed. She warns that interventions will not succeed unless they touch people at the level of self and supply a new definition and meaning to the idea of self.

Ronald Taylor reports on the family, school experience, and peer group relationships of young black males. He points out the exodus of social buffers from the inner city, and the ensuing spatial concentration of poverty. In this context, he suggests, a subculture of disengagement has developed, in which there are limited opportunity-providing social structures, a growing disarray in the socializing environment in general, and a paucity of positive role models. He finds a rational but ultimately dysfunctional disparity in how mothers raise their daughters and their sons which, he observes, must be related to the absence of the father in so many instances. He also finds the school experience particularly destructive in its effect, and says that, in light of these forces, the immense power of peer groups is an understandable consequence. He does note, however, the phenomenon of the "super kid," the young person who makes it in spite of all the negative stimuli he experiences.

The essays as a group lay powerful stress on the critical importance of what happens in adolescence in determining a person's life prospects. They make clear that a major function of adolescence is "connecting," and that if the larger society does not enable the connecting process to occur, it will not work properly. They paint a stark picture of the poor "connections" that exist for significant segments of America's adolescent population, with cumulative impact on longer-term education and employment prospects and performance.

There is hope in the essays, though. Leverage is possible, given the dynamic nature of adolescence. Two-thirds of poor adolescents do escape poverty. Parental attitudes and expectations can overcome the fact of poverty in a household in determining whether a youngster is able to escape. Where parents are not present or, if present are either inadequate or destructive, other adults can be helpful though not perfect substitutes. Teachers, older adolescents, and even program staff can build the strong, healthy relationships that all teenagers need. They can nurture and teach effectively, if they connect with the adolescent early enough and thoroughly enough.

The challenges are difficult. Especially with regard to those teens in environments of extreme, concentrated poverty such as the inner city, the essays imply that incremental change will not do. The authors present challenges that require a sense of urgency and a commitment to do things quite differently in a number of arenas. We hope the volume will indeed stimulate a new public debate to that end.

GROWING UP IN AMERICA

Robert Coles

LONG AGO—WHEN MY WIFE, Jane, and I were working with the black and white children who were initiating school desegregation against great odds in the early 1960s South—I was told something, tersely, by a black mother in Atlanta who clearly comprehended my effort to understand not only how her children were growing up, but how their psychological development, their personal growth, compared with the way white boys and girls were growing up, then, in Georgia: "You're the doctor, not me—but I'll tell you what I think; I think it's the same, but it's different." She stopped there, and I remember waiting for more, for an explanation, perhaps. But she had said as much as she wanted to say—and upon reflection, I began to realize she had given me a shrewd, telling summary of sorts: yes, all children have certain tasks to accomplish that go with growing up—but, then, the social and racial and national and regional background of a particular child can be extremely important, and can carry its own weight in this life.

Her remark still comes to mind, twenty-five years later, as I do my work in this country, and try to make sense of how boys and girls grow up here. On the one hand, I know that I have never met a child who, in a certain fashion, and at his or her own speed, doesn't try to strike out for a certain independence from a parent, from relatives, while at the same time needing their love, or in its absence, missing it sorely. On the other hand, I have never known a child who somehow doesn't have to come to terms with certain special circumstances (how to grow up rich or poor, black or white, in the South or the North) and so doing, learn how to say goodbye to the years of childhood dependency and vulnerability in a special manner that is distinctly shaped by those circumstances.

Moreover, history has its own bearing on our lives. The black child and the white child whom I will soon enough present to the reader

9

are by no means representative of most American children. Many black children have mothers who are jobless; many white children belong to families in which both parents work, and rely upon day-care (often of a less than ideal kind) rather than a family maid. Indeed, since I began my work with black and white families, in the 1960s, enormous changes have taken place on both sides of a racial line: higher unemployment among ghetto residents; a rising inci-dence of drug abuse, accompanied by growing criminality; schools that don't seem able to connect in important educational and psycho-logical ways with the children who are supposed to attend them. Meanwhile, many white children, even from well-off families, are lucky to see their parents in the evening for an hour or so—never mind have a maid to call upon, as is the case in the story about to be told. Still, what these witnesses soon to speak have to offer us, no matter some of the particulars of their lives, is the universality of their perceptions with respect to matters of race and class in this country, the glimpse they give us at what children think about themselves and their prospects, and how such matters of self-regard are given shape by the neighborhood world to which they belong.

Let me, right away, try to be as concrete as possible—to be so with the help of a woman who surely qualifies by knowledge and experi-ence as an "expert" with respect to a subject matter abstractly called, these days, "child development." She is forty years old and in her own way has been carrying on "cross-cultural research" in that "field" of child development for many years, though with no big deal grants from a federal agency or a foundation. Every day, six days a week, she observes closely how an affluent, white family's two children grow up, and every day she also observes closely how the three children of a relatively humble black family, her own, grow up. When I asked her to describe in a general way the results of her research, she told me this: "When I come here in the morning, to work, I go to the kitchen, and I get the kettle going, and that's when I talk with myself. I say: you're here, and not with your own kids, and that's the difference, right there. These [white] kids can have what they want. They've got the money. They've got the world smiling on them. They've got me, waiting on them. They speak; someone listens. They cough; someone comes running. They get annoyed, someone gets nervous. I hear the little girl talk about what she's going to do now, what she's going to do later, and where she's been, and where she'll be going, and I say to myself: she's only six, and she's already lived a nicer life, and been to more places, than me, and my mother, and when I remember that I have a daughter who's her age, then I either sit down and cry, or I want to tear up the whole house [where she works], or I just say my old prayer to God: 'Please, Jesus, help me along; help me to keep going,' because there are times when I'm ready to give up.

"I was asking the boy [aged eleven] how he's doing at school. He's a nice fellow; he's polite to me. He said he was doing just fine. He said he's got to write a report about some subject, what's happening to the land [ecology], and he's worried that the planet is in trouble. I thought it sure must be terrible, the way he's talking. He kept telling me things, and then he asked me if I was worried, too. I told him I guess I was, but he wanted me to get as upset as he was, I could tell. It seems like they have this home by the ocean, and the water is washing away some of the land, and they think in fifty years, they could be in big, big trouble. They're thinking of selling their home. Maybe they will buy another one, or they'll buy an island someplace, I heard them say. I'm supposed to cry, you know, when I hear them talk like that— I'm supposed to think the world is coming to an end, and it's awful, the way they think. Of course, five minutes later they're on to their next problem: which car is the best one to buy? She'll talk about leather seats and gas that's diesel, and he'll talk about how fast the car goes, and they worry about what the 'right' car to own is, and I don't know what they mean—whether it's 'right' meaning a good buy, or 'right,' meaning the neighbors will like it, or 'right,' meaning the car won't be bad for the 'environment.'

"When I hear them talking about 'environment,' I think of where we live. I wish they'd get all upset about our neighborhood [a public housing 'project'], our 'environment.' I wish they'd want to get rid of the rats and the garbage that has no place to go, and the lead poisoning the kids get, and all the drugs. The way it is, the police are friends with the drug folks, and my kids look out the window on a nice, sunny day, and they say: nope, I don't want to go out! My mother has been robbed and robbed, even with her white hair. There's no one safe. Here, everyone is safe—and there's other places they go visit, and they are safe, and that's the difference.

"The other day my boy told me he never wanted to grow up. I asked him why. He said, 'You grow up, and you die.' I said: 'Jason, everyone will die.' He said: 'Momma, some sooner and some later and here any second.' I told myself: 'Clara, you've got an educated eleven year old, who is smart enough to know what's ahead, so now what do you say?' I didn't know the answer. I just went on with my cooking. Lord, I was tired—a whole day with 'them'; and there I was, trying to get the energy to hold up my head and try to do good by my own three [children], and for a second I was ready to shout up to the Lord: 'You try again; you try again—and make this a better world, the next time around. Make it a place where people are more equal with each other, and there isn't the rich folks, a few, and they have everything, and the poor folks, lots of us, and there's little we have and little we can expect to have, ever.' That's a long speech to make—for the Lord to hear. Who am I to be telling Him anything? But you hear in church that He likes us, He said, and not the rich folks, so maybe one day it'll all be turned around, and we won't be rich, no sir, but our kids won't be afraid to grow up, like Jason is, and the rich kids won't be sitting on so much in life that they're running around and around in circles, and then you hear them saying that they're having a hard time making up their minds about what to buy and what they should do next!"

She has said more, much more. But in the above comments, extracted from a number of conversations, and edited for the sake of a concise narrative presentation, one finds so very much to consider with respect to growing up in America now, toward the end of the 20th century—the way class and race give shape to a family's sense of what is possible, what is impossible, what can be imagined, what is beyond the realm, even, of fantasy. That last matter, fantasy, is a rather more important one than might be thought. It is easy to document the many sociological and economic distinctions between the poor and the rich—describe the world of a ghetto, the world of a well-to-do suburb. It isn't so hard to compare the schools in a ghetto as against those in a suburb—the differences with respect to the appearance of the schools, the books and desks and walls and halls inside, the grounds outside, not to mention the atmosphere in the classrooms, the curriculum, the size of the class, the experience and training of the teachers. It is not all that hard to hear the children in each school talk—and thereby hear two altogether different languages, sets of assumptions, hopes, expectations. But inside the mind of every child is an ultimate truth of sorts—what a particular boy or girl thinks about, dreams about, in the course of a day, a night. To some extent, drawings and paintings of children help us gain access to that inner life of children—to day-dreams and reveries and so-called "idle" or "passing" thoughts, as rendered through crayons and paint brushes into a series of images. But children can't, obviously, put down on paper—through word or picture—the ever so many fantasies that cross their minds, only to give way to others. Only after a fairly long acquaintance do they sometimes begin to talk somewhat freely about what runs through their minds, as with adults.

Here, for instance, is Jason speaking in a relatively free-wheeling way. That is to say, I haven't been grabbing at him with pointed questions, and haven't been working hard to give focus and coherence to his stated opinions. We'd simply been gabbing—talking about what had happened during the week, what he'd seen on television, what he'd noticed on his way to school, what he had heard in the corridors of that school, and on the streets near the tenement house that is his house: "I was sitting in school [at his desk] and I remembered I saw on TV that they'd taken these pictures of some planet out there, and there were circles around it and moons, I think. I remembered "Star Wars." I thought: hey, Jason, leave this place, and wing your way to that planet. Maybe you could start something there! Maybe you could explore, and there'd be gold in a cave, [something] like that. Maybe you could find a place and build a house, and you'd have plenty of land, and there'd be no one bothering you! Trouble is, I know you'd be away, far away, and I don't know if you can breathe the air up over there.

"Lots of times I think: there must be some place that you can go, and no one is bothering you, and telling you 'watch out or we'll get you.' I was looking out the window the other day, and I saw these birds flying, and they didn't stop. Why should they? If I had wings, I'd take off and find me another spot where I could be—I don't know where.

"On TV I saw a race, a car race. I thought: 'Jason, you could be in one of those [cars], and just floor it, and don't turn around—just keep going zoom, zoom, until you see a nice place, then slow down, and go off the main road, and see if you can make friends with the people. You might not be able to—but they might like looking at the car. So, you let them. Maybe, you offer them a ride. Kids would like that! Then, they'll smile, maybe, and they might let you camp out some place and you could do that, and no one would slit your throat or pump you [with bullets]. You could walk, and you could go to some place and buy food, and they'd sell to you, and you'd be all set. If you got a job, you could stay there, if they let you. There'd be the cash to buy food. If you slept outside, there'd be no rent [to pay]. You could just enjoy yourself, and not have to look every way while you're walking. That would be a great time—to have lots of room, and not feel someone is out to get you, and you don't know why, so you'd better run all the time when you step outside. I wouldn't mind living alone on one of those planets, to tell you the truth. I think I'd enjoy myself, exploring around, and seeing if I could find myself a nice place to live. Like a bird does—build a nest!"

As I listen to such a boy day-dreaming out loud, I notice not only his subject matter, but the way he puts things, the constantly tentative or qualified nature of his statements, the urgency of his fantasies, and their obvious connection to the everyday reality of his life, no matter their vividly extra-terrestrial nature. This is a boy who yearns for a decent, safe world in which he may grow up; this is a boy whose view of his future very much determines his sense of what is possible or useful or worth trying now, in the day-to-day present of his life. Every child wonders what will happen in the years ahead—and as one hears children speculate or let their minds wander ahead in time, the truth of their present-day situation becomes all too evident.

Here, in contrast, is the vision of the ten-year-old boy whom Jason's mother attends as a maid and cook, five or six days a week, depending on the week: "I would like to be a lawyer. I'm interested in travel, and you can be a lawyer here [in Boston], and fly to London or Paris and work there sometimes. I'm not good in science in school, but I really like history. I like geography, too. A lot of the countries we study— I've been to them! My favorite is Switzerland. I've gone skiing there. It's real good—great slopes!

"What do I just think about sometimes? [I had asked.] I don't know—about trips we've taken, or going skiing, or sailing; about where I'll be going to school next, or what we'll do on the weekend. We go to Maine, and we take walks, and we spend the holidays there [at his family's summer home]. I think of driving—what kind of car I'll get. I'd like to have a sports car! But that's a few years off! I'd like to get a new bike soon. I like to ride my bike with my friends. We go and get ice creams. It's real fun! The man knows us [in the ice cream store], and he lets us charge it. I think he sends my mom the bill! I like to go out to eat with my parents. When it's Sunday [the 'maid' is off duty] we go out to eat. My mother can really cook good food, when she wants to, but a lot of the time she's tired, and she says: 'let's try some good restaurant'—and we do. We vote! We all say where we want to go, and a majority vote wins. We keep on voting until someplace wins the most votes!"

Such a pleasant, reassuring, promising world—the opportunities, the possibilities, the choices, the constant alternatives that arrive at this boy's door. He has his down moments, as do we all, but in no time there is a world that nods, beckons, says yes in a substantive way. One person in that world, of all ironies, is Jason's mother. She irons this well-off boy's clothes, cooks for him, serves him food on demand. "He rings and I run," she once told me, as terse and yet powerful a remark as I've ever heard, a statement of what class, finally, means in the lives of people, a statement worth dozens of social science textbooks. Nor is the issue only the confines and limitations, the learned subservience, that such a comment obviously reveals. A boy of ten who has grown accustomed to such personal authority over another, older human being has his own moral ambiguity, if not jeopardy to comprehend. Here is an excerpt from a conversation I held in 1985 with an eighteen-year-old college student of mine, presumably someone just about grown up: "I've had it so easy I don't really know if I could survive if I had to live like a lot of people do. When I wanted something [while growing up] I got it. When I needed something—or someone—all I had to do was say so. I wasn't spoiled rotten, no; my parents are decent folks, and they want us to think of others, and to work hard. But I'll tell you, they always made sure we had everything. We were waited on. We were taken all over the world. We were told that what we wanted out of life—well, we could have it. Now, I'm here [at college], and I've met people who have been struggling all their lives to get here, and they aren't sure where they'll be going, even though they're smart, and they work hard, because they just don't have the confidence I have. That's the word—you have confidence, because you've experienced the kind of life that inspires it. But there are days when I see people trying to take on the world, and I know the odds they face, and I realize how tough they are, and determined, and I'll begin to think they are the ones who really have confidence, and I'm just some lucky guy who whistles a nice tune, but I've never really been tested, and I'm spoiled, really spoiled, not the way some kids are, whose parents indulge them all the time, but by my life: things keep coming my way and falling my way. I guess I'll live my life like that; but the other day I was sitting and thinking, and I decided I'm living on some protected island, and maybe it's unreal, and maybe I'm as ignorant and disadvantaged in my own way—not like the poor, but in a different way."

Such a frankly self-critical moment is not all that common for many of us—who are quite content to take all we can get, worry little about others, less fortunate, and the devil with the consequences. That college freshman's sense of entitlement was qualified by a gnawing worry not only about the lives of others, far more vulnerable than he, but about his own future life—its potential insularity, its blind-spots, its temptation to self-centeredness, smugness, self-importance, and in a decisive way, its serious risk of blindness. In that last regard, here is a further moment of reflection by the same youth: "There's so much I've seen of the world! There's so much I know! But there's also a lot I don't know—I'll never know. I know my own small world—where everyone is really well off and has a good education. Capital, that's the word: capital that's there, and will stay there! What do 'we' know about 'them'—well, we know some of 'them,' because they work for us, and if we're halfway decent people, we're nice to them. But we don't know how they live, and I guess we don't really care. They have to know how we live—boy, do they! They watch our every move, and they're a step ahead of us, they have to be, it's their job. But we go whistling Dixie through life, and we're blind, deaf and dumb to them as people. They're not people for us the way we are for each other. They're servants, someone waiting on us in a store or a restaurant. That's what I've been thinking, lately—how ignorant you can be, even though you're very well educated, and you've gone to the best schools and got the best [SAT] scores. You don't know about how the huge majority of people live; you don't know what it's like to grow up and there's very little you own or you can take for granted. You're cut off in your own ghetto! I told my dad that the last time I went home [on a school break], and he thought I was losing my mind. 'What do you mean?' He asked me that, and he's a nice guy; he wasn't being angry, and he didn't want to argue. He just hadn't thought of all those others, the hundreds and hundreds of millions of people who live outside of our tight little island of a world!"

Such voices, those of the privileged and those of the ordinary working people of this country, remind us that even as we are one nation in certain respects, we are also many nations—and similarly with our children: they are boys and girls who, by the millions, share a common biological and psychological destiny, in that, step by step, they move toward adulthood; but they are also boys and girls who do so with particular hopes and fears, ambitions and hesitations which are no mere incidental or accidental aspect of their lives. On the contrary, we are, rather significantly, the offspring not only of our parents as the providers of our genes, but as the individuals who have a life to offer us—a residence here, a school there, a bank account in this neighborhood, or indeed, no bank account anywhere. A black woman who waits all day on a white child, while her own children fend for themselves—while an ailing grandmother tries the bet she can to help—is not quite in a position to offer those children what her employers offer their children. Still, that black woman has her own way of being tough, determined savvy, and not least, quite awake morally, alert socially. She tries to encourage her children, prod them vigorously and yet with sensitivity. Her children, given motivation and ability, can most certainly "move on up in the world," as their mother exhorts them to do. There are considerable difficulties, however—the grim neighborhood environment, the dismal school environment that is their inheritance, and that beclouds their child-hood years. In contrast, those of us who (as it is put in the South) do "right well" can find ways of enabling our children to follow suit, even when those children aren't all that spectacularly motivated in school, or able as students. Once, as I talked with the maid I have brought to this essay as an advisor, she phrased the similarities and differences between her son and that of her boss this way: "My Jason, he'd better

learn to be Superman, to break free of all the troubles waiting on him
around every corner. Their boy [the son of her employers], he can
smile and wink his way past any trouble that might come his way,
because he's got wings on him, even if he's not Superman himself,
and so if you have the wings, you fly, and that's what comes natural
to you, and if you don't, you've got to try becoming Superman, and
there's not many who can, and that's the difference."

So it goes, and so it has gone in the past. Needless to say, we in
America can have a collective, national dream—we can imagine a
future for our children in which differences do, indeed, obtain,
differences that have to do with temperament and talent, but not
differences that make for the grandest of opportunities for just about
everyone in one set of circumstances, and the slimmest of chances for
almost all in another set of circumstances. The point is not that all
children don't share certain, common experiences. They most certainly experience (almost all of them, save those terribly stunted) a
growing sense of awareness, a growing sense of what their minds and
bodies can do. They almost all experience the slow growth of individ-
uality and independence that marks off a young adult from a child—
the pleasure of becoming significantly someone on his or her own,
even though, of course, there are ties of varying degree of intensity
to various others. But for years we grow up not only in a home with
parents, but in a neighborhood with friends and people who live
nearby and schools we attend and playgrounds where we meet others,
learn our own version of a language, our own version of what it
means to be an American. This latter world is more significant in the
psychological and moral development of children than has often been
acknowledged by some of us social scientists and physicians—the way
in which, for instance, our attitudes toward school, toward teachers
are shaped by our expectations of what awaits us around the corner,
as we become grown up, or yes, what does not await us. Year after
year I have met children such as Jason, who hasn't an easy life ahead,
or his counterpart, who has such bright prospects; and gradually I
have come to realize that such children not only take in or absorb
their parents' psychology, their outlook, mannerisms, conflicts, but
take in a whole social and cultural climate: a particular experience of
what it means to be alive in a particular country at a particular
moment in its national life. "All children go through childhood,"
Anna Freud once said, acknowledging the obvious, but then she
added: "But that is only the beginning of things, because there are
dozens of ways for them to travel, and we must learn what those
different ways entail for the young travellers." My hunch is that the
humble maid whom I have quoted earlier is a handy guide for us, as
valuable an observer as any available to us.

THE LOGIC OF ADOLESCENCE

Laurence Steinberg

THE LOGIC OF ADOLESCENCE is revealed in the origins of the word. Derived from a Latin verb, *adolescere*—to grow into maturity—the term adolescence connotes both a process and a purpose. Fundamentally, we view adolescence as a period of transition, of movement and change, rather than as a static time in the individual life span. By its very nature, adolescence is a period of preparation, defined less by its own essence than by what it is followed by—maturity.

The psychosocial agenda of this period of preparation is shaped by a combination of forces, some universal and some particular to a given time and place. The universal features of adolescence are the elements of process, such as biological maturation and cognitive growth, that instigate change and impel the young person toward the purpose of maturity. The particular features of adolescence—the specific economic, cultural, and social circumstances under which a young person or a cohort of young people come of age—are what provide the purpose in any specific period of time, however. They dictate the definition of psychosocial maturity, structure the pathways through which maturity is pursued, and determine in large measure whether the pursuit is successful. No discussion of the logic of adolescence is complete without a consideration of both sets of elements.

This chapter explores the logic of adolescence in contemporary society both as a prelude to adulthood and as a developmental period of significance in its own right. What is distinctive about adolescence as a period in the life cycle? What do we hope our young people will accomplish during the second decade of life? How does the structure of contemporary society facilitate or impede the goals we set?

It begins with an overview of several universal features of the adolescent transition, followed by a very brief outline of the developmental tasks of adolescence. Finally, the nature of adolescence in contemporary society is discussed and several distinctive aspects of adolescence today are examined. Against this backdrop, we return to the psychosocial agenda and consider ways in which developmental tasks, and their negotiation in contemporary America, are shaped by the larger social forces in young people's lives. In this context, the question of how the agenda and its negotiation may be different for youngsters growing up under disadvantaged circumstances is specifically addressed.

UNIVERSAL FEATURES OF THE ADOLESCENT TRANSITION

Biological Maturation

In all mammalian species, adolescence is the period during which reproductive maturity is attained. The physical changes leading up to this attainment, collectively labelled *puberty*, are manifested in five observable phenomena: a rapid acceleration in growth, resulting in dramatic increases in height and weight; the further development of the gonads, or sex glands; the development of so-called "secondary sex characteristics," including changes in the genitals and breasts, the growth of pubic, facial, and body hair, and the further development of the sex organs; changes in the distribution of fat and muscle; and changes in the circulatory and respiratory systems, which lead to increased strength and tolerance for exercise.[1] Puberty is set in motion by a series of changes in the endocrine and central nervous systems, many of which begin several years before the external signs of puberty are evident.

Several aspects of human pubertal maturation make it especially important to the psychosocial agenda of adolescence. First, and perhaps most obvious, is the relation between pubertal maturation and sexual activity. The hormonal changes of puberty both increase the individual's sex drive and lead ultimately toward adult reproductive capability—the biological readiness of the individual to impregnate, or to become pregnant. Although children may be capable of experiencing sexual arousal and pleasurable sexual feelings, they are not as aware as adolescents of sexual impulses or of their own sexual desires. And because of the fact that the postpubertal adolescent is capable of becoming pregnant or fathering a child, the nature and meaning of sexual activity takes on profound additional importance both for the individual and for society.

A second aspect of puberty that makes it especially significant is its salience, or felt importance. At no other time in the human life cycle after infancy is growth more rapid, and at no other time is it more salient to the individual and those around him or her. The growth spurt and the development of secondary sex characteristics, in particular, transform the individual's self-concept, relations with agemates, and interactions with parents and other adults. Individuals may feel older because they look older, may be invited to engage in "older" types of activities with their friends because of their more adult-like appearance, and may be responded to differently by adults who equate changes in outward appearance with changes in internal motives and capabilities.[2] One effect of the salience of physical changes associated with puberty is the tendency (and, at times, the danger) of extrapolating from the physical to the psychological: There is no one-to-one correspondence between the external appearance of the adolescent and his or her psychological capability or motives, but both the individual and those around him or her frequently assume that there is such a correspondence.

A final important aspect of the elements of puberty concerns their variability between and within individuals. All adolescents do not begin puberty at the same age, pass through the changes at the same rate, or complete physical maturation at the same time. As a consequence, a group of youngsters the same chronological age—a class of seventh-graders, for instance—will vary markedly in physical status, with some reaching adult physical maturity before their peers have even begun the pubertal process. Even within one individual, there is considerable "asynchronicity" in growth—the secondary sex characteristics do not all appear at once, nor does menarche (the beginning of menstruation) necessarily coincide with the growth spurt. There is some evidence that early adolescence, especially for girls, may be a time of heightened vulnerability to psychological distress, some of which may be instigated by the biological changes of the period.[3]

Having highlighted the significance of puberty with regard to its sexual implications, its salience, and its variability, it is important as well to point out several ways in which puberty is *less* important than is widely assumed. First, there is no evidence whatsoever that the internal hormonal changes of adolescence are linked in any direct way to fluctuations in adolescents' mood or morale. If adolescents are moody, oppositional, or difficult, it is not because of "raging hormones." For one thing, many of the hormonal changes of adolescence are not "raging"; they are gradual, and begin, in fact, long before the period of putative difficulty. For another, the links between hormones and behavior in humans are quite complex, and mediated to large measure by environmental circumstances[4]. For a third, and to the surprise of most adults, there is little evidence that adolescents feel substantially more moody or psychologically troubled than either children or adults.[5] They may irritate adults more than children or other adults do, but this probably says more about what bothers adults than it does about the behavior of teenagers.

Finally, attempts to link biological changes at adolescence with cognitive changes have proven largely futile. As is the case with feelings, there is no simple relation between hormones and intellect. This comes as a surprise to many who believe that early adolescence is, by its biological nature, a period that schools must simply endure, since individuals are more or less "unteachable." Similarly, although several different biologically-based theories have been postulated to account for sex differences in adolescents' performance in school and on various intellectual tests, none has received much empirical support.[6]

Cognitive Maturation

Along with puberty, the cognitive changes of the period provide another universal in the adolescent experience. Not only do teenagers know more than children, but adolescents actually think in ways that are more advanced, more efficient, and generally more effective. This is seen in three chief ways. First, in adolescence the individual's ability to think about the possible in addition to the real increases markedly. The adolescent's thinking is less bound to concrete events than is the child's, and is, therefore, increasingly oriented toward past and future as well as to the present. Second, the adolescent is better able to engage in hypothetical, or "if-then," thinking. This is a powerful cognitive tool, since it permits the adolescent to anticipate the logical consequences of his or her actions without actually having to engage in them and to formulate elegant after-the-fact explanations for things that have occurred. Finally, with adolescence comes the ability to think in sophisticated ways about abstract concepts, including the process of thinking itself. Adolescents find it easier than children to comprehend the sort of higher-order, abstract logic inherent in puns, metaphors, and analogies. They are far more interested than are children in matters ideological, philosophical, psychological, and political. And they are far more given to self-scrutiny, introspection, and self-consciousness.[7]

Several implications of these cognitive changes for the psychosocial agenda of adolescence are noteworthy. Many of the most important consequences of the cognitive maturation characteristic of adolescence are social in nature. The logical sophistication of the adolescent is played out not only in the classroom, but in his or her social relations as well. If crises over identity, intimacy, or independence come to the fore in adolescence, it is partly due to the increased capability of the individual to ponder, and worry about, such concerns.

As is the case with puberty, however, there are substantial differences between and within individuals in the timing, rate, and extent of the development of sophisticated thinking. Much of the variability, we think, is attributable to differences in environmental stimulation. While adolescence brings with it the potential to mature intellectually, this potential is more often realized in youngsters who have the benefits of stimulating home, school, and extracurricular environments.

Finally, it is important to say something about the limitations of adolescent reasoning, since they may underlie some of the more curious and puzzling aspects of adolescent behavior. The limitations meant here are those referred to by psychologists as elements of "adolescent egocentrism," and they occur in part because of a mismatch between cognitive expansion and day-to-day experience.[8] Adolescent egocentrism appears to emerge early in adolescence and recedes with age and experience. In a manner of speaking, the young adolescent temporarily may be "too smart" for his or her own good.

Two components of adolescent egocentrism are especially noteworthy. The first is the *imaginary audience phenomenon*, a type of heightened self-consciousness. The adolescent who, on her way to a rock concert, feels that an entire arena of teenagers will notice her clothes is exhibiting imaginary audience behavior in its classic form. The fact that adolescents engage in imaginary audience behavior has serious implications for understanding adolescent misbehavior, because it suggests at least one reason for teenagers' special susceptibility to peer influence. All adolescents, of course, worry about how they are viewed by their friends and classmates, and attempt to behave in ways that will enhance their acceptance. But by creating an imaginary audience of their peers, adolescents accentuate the effect of this phenomenon. Adolescents thus are likely to overestimate the degree to which their behavior will lead to social acceptance or social rejection.

A second element of adolescent egocentrism is the emergence of a *personal fable*. The personal fable derives from the adolescent's erroneous belief that his or her experiences are unique. In effect, the heightened self-consciousness of the young adolescent can lead to feelings of exaggerated self-importance. For example, many teenagers engage in behaviors that they "know" are risky because they hold onto the personal fable that they themselves are not as susceptible to the risks as is everyone else. Thus, an adolescent who fully understands what causes pregnancy, or how to prevent conception, may have unprotected intercourse because she actually believes that *she* will not become pregnant.

THE DEVELOPMENTAL TASKS OF ADOLESCENCE

Because the central purpose of adolescence in all societies is the preparation of young people for maturity, the psychosocial agenda of necessity is defined by society's requirements for adulthood. In all societies, these requirements generally revolve around three sets of tasks: those involving love, those involving work, and those involving social responsibility. The mature adult is expected to have the capacity to form and maintain caring and gratifying relationships with others (including, but not limited to, mates and offspring); to attain the skills, motives, and interests necessary to contribute to and take pleasure in society's activities of production and leisure; and to acquire the values and concerns necessary to contribute to the well-being of the community.

The immediate developmental tasks of adolescence reflect these long-range goals. In order to enter adulthood equipped to engage in mature and satisfying relationships with others, participate in activities of production and leisure, and embrace the responsibilities of community, the adolescent must first resolve a series of preparatory psychosocial issues.

One set of issues concerns *intimacy and interpersonal responsibility*, including the ability to form satisfying emotional attachments to others that are characterized by sensitivity, mutuality, responsibility, and trust. Much interpersonal development continues to take place after adolescence, but we expect that most young people enter adulthood able to "connect" with other people and function adequately in group situations. These capabilities are important in forming and maintaining healthy familial relationships, of course, but the development of the capacity to relate to others in mature ways is important in other domains, too. Indeed, as our economy has become increasingly more service-oriented, interpersonal competence has taken on new and special significance as a prerequisite for labor market success.

A second set of issues concerns *identity and personal responsibility*, including the development of a coherent and positive sense of self and the ability to make informed decisions, exercise judgment, and regulate one's own behavior appropriately. Modern societies, in particular, because they leave to the individual so many choices about behavior and lifestyle, demand that individuals be able to evaluate alternative courses of action and select among them intelligently. Such decisions ultimately depend on self-assuredness, self-knowledge, and clarity of purpose. As is the case with interpersonal competence, we know that much development in the realms of identity and self-governance continues into and throughout adulthood. But young people who move through adolescence confused (rather than merely undecided) about who they are, hesitant (rather than simply modest) about their abilities, and submissive (rather than cautious) in the face of pressure from others are at a distinct disadvantage relative to their peers, and they are less able to make use of institutional resources that society provides to help adolescents make a more fruitful transition into adulthood.

A final set of issues on the psychosocial agenda of adolescence concerns *achievement and social responsibility*, including the development of the basic skills, knowledge, and capabilities needed to participate successfully in the work and educational institutions of young adulthood, and the development of a personal system of values and beliefs that will provide a basis for socially responsible behavior and lay the groundwork for active participation in the community. It is difficult to specify what the "educated" adolescent ought to know before entering adulthood—as ongoing debates over such issues as national educational standards and core curricula attest. Yet most of us can surely agree that the competent adolescent should be fluent enough with language, logic, and numbers to be able either to secure gainful employment or to satisfy the entrance requirements for an institution of higher education; proficient enough in so-called "life skills" to be capable of self-sufficiency; and knowledgeable enough about our culture and civilization to participate adequately in activities of citizenship and leisure. As well, an important part of preparing for adulthood is the development of a system of values and beliefs that permit the individual to make ethical and moral decisions and behave in a socially responsible fashion. Again, this is not to say that development in these areas will not continue after adolescence but, rather, that a level of proficiency sufficient for autonomous functioning should be achieved prior to the beginning of adulthood.[9]

The biological and cognitive maturation of the individual provide both the impetus for taking on these psychosocial tasks and the equipment needed to negotiate them successfully. With respect to biology, the physical changes of puberty transform the adolescent's relations with others, self-conceptions, and capabilities, and these transformations reverberate in the realms of intimacy, identity, and achievement. The physically mature adolescent is now ready (as well as motivated) to experiment with intimacy, with self-reliance, and with adult responsibilities. Logical maturation acts in comparable ways—as both a catalyst and a tool. The individual who can better take the perspective of others is interested in, and capable of, more intense relationships; one who can systematically envision his or her future is eager and able to get on with the work of identity development; the young person who has intellectual muscle is both ready and willing to exercise it.[10]

The successful resolution of the developmental tasks of adolescence, however, is only partly dependent on the child's biological and intellectual readiness. Puberty and abstract thinking place the child on the road toward adult psychosocial maturity. Whether the journey is smooth or rocky, and ultimately, whether it is successful or not, however, depends on the social context in which the child comes of age. The effects of biological maturation on the child's psychological development, for example, will be different in a society (or a community or a family) in which puberty is celebrated than in one in which it is greeted with trepidation. Similarly, the impact of intellectual maturation on the adolescent will depend on the opportunities society affords the young person to exercise abstract thinking and on the extent to which such logical sophistication is an asset or liability. In other words, although biological and cognitive maturation are universal instigators of psychosocial development in adolescence, their effects are moderated by the social ecology in which they occur.

DISTINCTIVE FEATURES OF ADOLESCENCE IN CONTEMPORARY SOCIETY

Sociological, historical, and anthropological writings tell us that adolescence as we know it today—and, consequently, the developmental tasks facing young people today—are particular products of our time and culture. Thus, while the charge in this chapter is to address psychological development during adolescence, it is impossible to do so without attending to the broader social context in which today's young people come of age. Adolescence has changed in many ways over time, but three distinctive features of contemporary adolescence seem of special significance.

Age Segregation and the Loss of Adult Protection

During the last 150 years, young people have become increasingly segregated from their elders.[11] As a consequence, they have become increasingly likely to spend their time in the exclusive company of agemates and less likely to enjoy the protection and supervision of adults. Changes in schooling, in the workplace, and in family life have all furthered the trend toward the separation of young from old. As a result, few young people in America today have even one significant, close relationship with a nonfamilial adult before reaching adulthood themselves. This is a very different state of affairs than existed even 100 years ago.

Consider first the impact that compulsory secondary education has had on adolescents' opportunities to interact with adults outside the family. During the 19th century, most young people left school early in adolescence, to begin work.[12] Today, in contrast, individuals enter educational institutions at the age of five or so—an increasingly larger proportion enter such institutions even earlier, in the form of day care or preschool—and remain divided into chronologically defined age groups until at least sixteen (and typically, eighteen). Daily contact with adults is limited, for the most part, to their own family members and the handful of teachers they encounter at school—teachers whom they encounter mainly in ratios of one to twenty-five. Although there are exceptions, most middle schools and high schools are impersonal institutions in which teenagers are unlikely to form meaningful relations with any adults.

Changes in the workplace have had similarly adverse effects on intergenerational relations. As work and family life became more separated, physically as well as economically, so did adolescents and adults. That industrialization limited young people's participation in the labor force as workers is well documented; although many students today hold part-time or summer jobs, when teenagers work, they do so in a distinctively adolescent segment of the labor force (e.g., in the fast food industry), in which relationships with adults are no more likely to form than in schools.[13] In addition, as work settings and households became physically separated, with work concentrated in urban settings and households in exurban and suburban neighborhoods, opportunities for young people to encounter adults in passing—on the way to and from school, during afternoon games and play, and so forth—grew scarce.

Whereas changes in school and work have isolated young people from adults in general, changes in the family, especially in the last twenty-five years, may have distanced young people even from their own parents. Today, more than 70 percent of all mothers with school-aged children are employed (the percentage is higher among single mothers and lower among married mothers).[14] Perhaps the most salient manifestation of this with respect to age-segregation is the so-called "latch-key" phenomenon: about 15 percent of all children between the ages of seven and thirteen care for themselves after school each day; most probably, the proportion of older adolescents in self-care after school is substantially higher, although precise estimates are not readily available.[15] Less well-studied are the effects that maternal employment has had on patterns of family interaction during morning hours, during weekday evenings, and on weekends. It is difficult to imagine, however, that it has increased the amount of time youngsters spend in the company of their parents.

Accompanying this increase in maternal employment have been increases in the rates of parental divorce and nonmarital childbearing, both of which have contributed to a dramatic increase in the proportion of adolescents residing in single-parent households. Approximately 60 percent of all young people spend some portion of their childhood or adolescence in a single-parent household, with an average length of time in such an arrangement of six years. About half of all young people experience parental divorce or separation before reaching adulthood. Although one may debate the effects that this change in family structure has on the adolescent's development, it is almost always the case that divorce diminishes the amount of contact the young person has with the noncustodial parent, typically the father. By two years after a divorce, most children living with their mother see their father rarely or not at all.[16]

This increase in segregation of adolescents from adults over the past century and a half has led to a gradual erosion of the protective cover that adolescents once enjoyed under the supervision of their elders. This protection formerly inhered in the more frequent contact young people had with adults in their communities, their work settings, and perhaps even their homes. Compared with that of his or her counterparts previously, the contemporary adolescent's daily routine is strikingly lacking in regular and meaningful contact with adult men and women who have a real stake in how that particular adolescent is socialized for the future. As schools have grown in size, so has students' sense of anonymity, and a large proportion report in surveys that they feel distant and isolated from their teachers. As the workplace has become segmented—into environments in which adults work and those in which adolescents work—opportunities for intergenerational contact outside home and school have diminished. And as family life has been transformed by maternal employment and marital disruption, occasions for adolescents to connect with their own parents have become fewer and more difficult to arrange. More than was the case in the past, today's adolescent must either go it alone or depend on the counsel of equally inexperienced agemates.

Adolescent Rolelessness and the Loss of Purpose

A second feature that distinguishes adolescence in contemporary society concerns the "rolelessness" of young people. Many commentators on the adolescent scene, drawing on historical and cross-cultural data, have remarked on the absence of satisfying roles for young people in contemporary society, especially in comparison to their counterparts of 150 years ago.[17] Lengthening the adolescent period through the extension of schooling and the concomitant prolongation of economic dependence on adults has left adolescents in quite a difficult situation. They possess many of the psychological, biological, and social skills to function as adult members of society but lack access to society's most meaningful roles and important resources. Although they are capable in many ways of making adult contributions to society, adolescents are not encouraged to do so, and in some regards, they actually are prohibited from doing so. Thus, not only have adolescents been segregated from adults, they have also been segregated from adult roles.

The problem of rolelessness has become especially troublesome for the nearly one-half of the adolescent population who do not pursue education beyond high school. Several decades ago, changes in the economy began to eliminate meaningful work roles for young people who had left high school before graduating. In recent years, the decline of employment opportunities in manufacturing and related sectors of the economy has begun to eradicate meaningful work roles for young people who complete the diploma, but do not or cannot progress into postsecondary education. Although we like to think of ourselves as a society that offers its youth a variety of alternative pathways to adulthood (perhaps this was true twenty-five years ago), this is hardly the case today. Quite the contrary: we have moved into an era in which the only meaningful role an adolescent can occupy in society is as a student, and the only pathway to successful adulthood is prolonged formal schooling. And, while there is not anything inherently wrong with the student role, it is clearly not well-suited for all young people. Not everyone has as real an opportunity to function well in the role of student, because being a successful student requires types of ability, degrees of motivation, and levels of affluence not uniformly distributed across the adolescent population.

Adolescence itself has become a social and economic holding period. It has been transformed from a stage in the life cycle characterized by active production to one dominated by passive consumption. But the consumer role, although superficially enjoyable, is neither psychologically nor existentially satisfying—it is a shopping spree that brings short-lived gratification but little lasting satisfaction. To the biologically and cognitively mature adolescent, who must punch the educational clock for what must seem like an endless period of years, the wait before getting on with the business of adulthood must seem interminable. For this reason, as suggested below, young people are impelled to find other ways to become adult.

Pseudomaturity and Heightened Risk

When considered alongside the picture of age-segregation described earlier, the rolelessness of contemporary youth points up a paradox about the nature of adolescence in contemporary society. Prior to the twentieth century, adolescence was a period of "semi-autonomy," in which adolescents worked and earned money but lived under the protective cover of adults in their community. Over the past 100 years, adolescents' access to legitimate adult roles has been increasingly constrained, while the protection that they once enjoyed by virtue of their close contact with adults has been gradually eroded by changes in the family and other social institutions. Thus, adolescents are both more and less autonomous today than they were in the past. Owing to age-segregation, contemporary teenagers are given a relatively high degree of freedom to pursue *adolescent* activities (for example, contemporary adolescents have more autonomy than did their counterparts previously in matters of leisure, discretionary consumption, and grooming). But owing to their rolelessness, they have relatively less autonomy to pursue societally-valued *adult* activities (it is more difficult for a young person today to secure full-time employment than it was early in this century, for example). In concrete terms, adolescents today may find it easier to purchase illicit drugs than to obtain legitimate employment.

The third feature of adolescence in contemporary society inheres in this irony. The specific combination of age-segregation and rolelessness has made adolescence a trivialized stage of life, in which the important task of preparation for adulthood has taken a back seat to entertainment, consumption, and frivolity.[18] Tired of waiting to get on with the work of adulthood, adolescents turn to leisure to fill the hours and sublimate their energies. Denied access to legitimate adult status, yet stimulated to grow up faster, young people are encouraged to direct their leisure activity toward acquiring the superficial trappings of age—to dress, spend, and recreate like adults—without developing (or before they have developed) the emotional and psychological maturity associated with adulthood. This has given rise to what has been called the "pseudomaturity" of youth.

That adolescence has been trivialized, stripped of authenticity, is not a fresh observation—it was made quite explicitly by Edgar Friedenberg thirty years ago in *The Vanishing Adolescent* (1959), and again in 1966 by Elizabeth Douvan and Joseph Adelson, in *The Adolescent Experience*. But the pseudomaturity of today's youth is both different from and potentially far more dangerous than it was in the past. During the 1950s and the early 1960s, pseudomaturity was a posture, an attitude captured in the television programs of the era, which portrayed adolescents as silly. Friedenberg worried about the "country-club" atmosphere of American high schools, Douvan and Adelson about the "mixed childishness and false adulthood" of the teen culture. Today, high schools still give off an air of clubbiness, with membership defined by designer sneakers, expensive jewelry, and foreign cars, and the teen culture of MTV and video parlors still reeks of an uncomfortable mixture of the naive and the corrupted. But today's version of pseudomaturity includes less understanding of the risks of behavior as well as questionable values, and therein lies the problem. Drug use and sexual intercourse, for example, are now part of the trappings of adulthood to which even young adolescents aspire, and engaging in these behaviors is now part of the "package" of behaving like, if not being, an adult.

When we consider these three historical changes in the nature of adolescence together—the erosion of adult protection, the disappearance of social purpose, and the rise of pseudomaturity and its attendant risks—the picture of metamorphosis that emerges is startling. At a point not all that long ago in our history, adolescence was a time during which young people, with the help of adults who had a genuine interest in their socialization, were gradually prepared for the work and family roles they would be expected to assume as adults. Adolescence was not a mixture of the childish and the adult, it was a stage with a logic and definition of its own. The status and purpose of the period were clear: adolescence was a period of semi-autonomy, of gradual transition, of preparation—preparation which occurred within the context of a protective network of relationships with immediate and extended family members, adults in the community, and workmates. Alternative pathways toward adulthood were available. For those with money and patience, schooling was the ticket. For those without one or the other, opportunities existed to get on with the business of adulthood on a faster timetable.

Today's adolescents face a different world indeed. They are less protected and less supervised by adults, and spend more time alone or in the company of their peers. Whether they want to or not—indeed, whether they are up to it or not—they are expected patiently and obediently to endure a prolonged period of schooling, anticipating adulthood from a distance, through television and film, rather than experiencing it firsthand. And they are tempted, each day, to experiment with some aspects of adulthood that are among the least important, and potentially most dangerous, things about growing up. It is in this context of diminished protection, cloudy purpose, and heightened risk that today's young person comes of age. This specific constellation has changed not only the nature of adolescence, but the nature of what it takes to negotiate the passage into maturity successfully.

Faced with the developmental agenda of adolescence in contemporary society, with its high demands for self-definition and autonomous functioning, today's young person must be able to find a protective niche in which to grow, while patiently enduring a lengthy period of schooling that has become a prerequisite to adult status. Along the way, adolescents must withstand constant encouragement from both agemates and the world around them to engage in behaviors that are dangerous—perhaps even life-threatening. To be successful in this context, the young person needs a combination of internal fortitude, social support, and a vision for his or her future.

COMING OF AGE IN CONTEMPORARY AMERICA: THE BIFURCATION OF ADOLESCENT EXPERIENCE

Although the basic elements of the developmental tasks of adolescence have remained constant over the past century, transformations in the nature of society have made their successful resolution more difficult for young people. As a consequence, more adolescents move into adulthood having failed to resolve the necessary developmental tasks adequately. It is difficult to document changes over time in psychosocial development, but when we look at various indicators of psychological and social pathology we can see quite clearly that young people have been showing signs of difficulty for some time now. Between 1950 and 1980, rates of social pathology among the young—

as indexed by such things as drug and alcohol use, suicide, criminal and violent behavior, nonmarital pregnancy, and academic failure—rose steadily, and although they peaked during the early 1980s, they have not fallen appreciably since that time.[19]

Unfortunately, high levels of social pathology, while discouraging enough, probably underestimate the true degree of psychosocial disruption among American youth. Suicide statistics do not reveal how many adolescents are profoundly or even mildly depressed. Arrest records underestimate the extent of true delinquency and provide only a very small window on less serious offenses, which go largely unreported. Most of the information on drug and alcohol use comes from surveys of high school seniors, but the age of initiation of drug use has been creeping downward steadily to involve the pre-high school years. Pregnancy statistics tell one side of the story, but they do not reveal much about the ignorance young people have about sex, or the tremendous pressure many youngsters feel to engage in sexual activities about which they feel uncomfortable. Reports of low achievement test scores and high drop-out rates do not tell us how many youngsters are bored, disinterested in school, or physically present in school but psychologically absent from the classroom.

It is difficult to document the causal processes behind these trends. Social scientists continue to debate the sources of the problem. But many observers of the adolescent scene believe that the particular combination of autonomy, rolelessness, and risk characteristic of adolescence in contemporary America has endangered the psychosocial development of young people and, as a result, the well-being of our society. Without the help of their elders, adolescents must find it difficult to acquire the interpersonal, personal, and social proficiencies necessary to function as mature adults. Without a sense of purposefulness, young people must find it difficult to chart or maintain a course for the future or invest in the institutions that will help them get there. And, with pressures to grow up faster—or at least to appear on the surface as if they have grown up—adolescents must find it virtually impossible to avoid becoming cynical, skeptical, confused, and jaded.

Lest we become too gloomy, however, we must not lose sight of the fact that most American youngsters manage to get along and move into adulthood without experiencing serious psychological or social disruption. By young adulthood, the vast majority have settled into socially-accepted patterns of work and family life. One of every ten adolescent girls gets pregnant before age twenty, but nine in ten do not. Twenty percent of students do not complete high school by the societally-expected age, but 80 percent do, and a substantial number of young people who leave school prematurely receive a high school diploma later. The majority of adolescents have experimented with alcohol and marijuana, but only a minority of teenagers develop substance abuse problems of any significance. It is always tempting for adults to lament the ignorance and decadence of the young, but the fact of the matter is that the current generation of young people will probably grow up to be adults who are, finally, not all that different from previous cohorts. In some regards, we should admire these young people, because they have survived—some have even flourished—within a psychosocially more hostile and difficult society than that known by their elders.

These are not reasons to be sanguine, to be sure, but it is important to bear in mind that a relatively small percentage of the adolescent population accounts for a relatively high proportion of serious problems seen in this age group. It seems clear, then, that one can not escape the conclusion that there are two adolescent experiences in contemporary America—two quite separate developmental trajectories. The majority of young people, despite occasional experimentations with deviance or flirtations with danger and despite less than ideal levels of adult contact and role definition, continue on in school, move into postsecondary institutions along a socially acceptable timetable, and enter into work and family commitments along a schedule that is not significantly different from their counterparts of forty years ago. On quite another trajectory, however, are those whose lives are compromised by academic failure, poor health, early childbearing, drug use, and unemployment. These youngsters enter adulthood, too, but their route leads to a far different destination from that reached by their more fortunate counterparts. It is an adulthood characterized, in far too many cases, by poverty, alienation and social deviance. And as we know, it is a fate that is far more likely to befall poor, inner-city, and minority youngsters than their more affluent, suburban, and majority agemates.

To the extent that autonomy, rolelessness, and risk among the young contribute to the genesis of psychosocial problems, it is not difficult to understand why some young people find themselves on one trajectory and not the other. Young people who grow up under conditions of disadvantage are far less protected than their peers, and they grow up in an environment that is far less forgiving. They are less likely to have opportunities for meaningful participation in society, less likely to envision themselves as having such opportunities as adults, and, understandably, less willing to embrace a role whose purpose is even less clear and whose rewards both more distant and

more uncertain than those facing advantaged youngsters. And, because they have so little else to aspire to, they are more easily tempted
by the instant gratification and pseudomaturity offered by substances
and behaviors that carry great danger.

In conclusion, to return to the starting point: what is the logic of
adolescence, and how has this logic been transformed in contemporary America? Although adolescence brings with it a particular psychosocial agenda, the extent to which youth negotiate the constituent
tasks successfully has little to do with the developmental givens of the
period per se. Ultimately, the successful transition from childhood
into adulthood inheres in the interaction between the developing
young adult, and the social context in which he or she is coming of
age. Becoming an adult is more difficult in today's society than it has
been in the past for all young people, but even more difficult for
some adolescents than for others.

Today's psychosocial agenda necessitates social (not just economic)
protection, purpose, and patience. Youth who have the guidance of
adults, who understand and accept the preparatory role of adolescence (and who have the affluence to afford the luxury of waiting),
and who are encouraged to forsake the temptations of adulthood for
the pleasures of youth itself are likely to find that the path toward
maturity can be a relatively smooth and satisfying one. Their peers
whose adolescent experience is characterized by excessive autonomy,
rolelessness, and risk will not be so fortunate. The conditions under
which these latter youngsters come of age clash with the very psychosocial agenda we expect them to accomplish. The context in which
they grow impedes their psychosocial development, heightens their
vulnerability to psychological and social pathology, and calls into
question the very logic of adolescence itself as it exists for them.

NOTES

1. W. Marshall, "Puberty," in F. Falkner and J. Tanner, eds. *Human Growth*
2 (New York: Plenum Press, 1978).

2. J. Brooks-Gunn and E. Reiter, "The Role of Pubertal Processes in the
Early Adolescent Transition," in S. Feldman and G. Elliott, eds., *At the
Threshold: The Developing Adolescent.* (Cambridge: Harvard University Press,
1990).

3. *Ibid.*

4. *Ibid.*

5. R. Larson and C. Lampman-Petraitis, "Daily Emotional States as Reported by Children and Adolescents," *Child Development* 60 (1989).

6. D. Keating, "Adolescent Thinking," in Feldman and Elliott, *At the Threshold.*

7. *Ibid.*

8. For an extended discussion of adolescent egocentrism, see D. Elkind, "Understanding the Young Adolescent," *Adolescence* 13, pp. 127–134.

9. For an extensive discussion of these issues, see E. Greenberger, "Defining Psychosocial Maturity in Adolescence," in P. Karoly and J. Steffen, eds., *Adolescent Behavior Disorders: Foundations and Contemporary Concerns,* (Lexington, MA: D.C. Heath, 1984).

10. L. Steinberg, *Adolescence* (2nd edition). (New York: Knopf, 1989).

11. U. Bronfenbrenner, "The Origins of Alienation," *Scientific American* 231 (1974): 53–81.

12. J. Katz, *Rites of Passage.* (New York: Basic Books, 1977).

13. E. Greenberger and L. Steinberg, *When Teenagers Work: The Psychological and Social Costs of Adolescent Employment.* (New York: Basic Books, 1986).

14. F. Furstenberg, "Coming of Age in a Changing Family System," in Feldman and Elliott, *At the Threshold.*

15. L. Steinberg, *Adolescence.*

16. F. Furstenberg, Jr., "Coming of Age."

17. President's Science Advisory Committee, *Youth: Transition to Adulthood.* (Chicago: University of Chicago Press, 1974).

18. E. Greenberger and L. Steinberg, *When Teenagers Work.*

19. A summary of recent trends appears in L. Steinberg, *Adolescence.*

THE ADOLESCENT POOR AND THE TRANSITION TO EARLY ADULTHOOD

Andrew M. Sum
W. Neal Fogg

OVER THE PAST FIFTEEN YEARS, the adolescent population of the United States declined by nearly four million persons, or 15 percent. Yet, despite this sharp drop in the total, the number living in poor families increased over the same period. During early 1988, nearly one of every five adolescents was a member of a family with an income below the poverty line.

Adolescence traditionally has been viewed by educators, psychologists, and sociologists as a formative period. This life stage includes critical "investment years" in educational and personal development, and in socialization. During these years, adolescents prepare themselves for further "human capital" building in post-secondary education, full-time participation in the labor market, and entry into adult society. During the 1980s, all these areas of investment—in academic skills, formal schooling, and work experience—became increasingly important in determining the economic success and overall life options of young adults in American society.

Over this period, the U.S. labor market was subject to a substantial degree of turbulence, and it was transformed in a number of substantive ways, with important consequences for the early school-to-work transition of the nation's non-college bound youth. Greater delays in access to career labor market jobs, and the disappearance of many well-paid, entry-level jobs in manufacturing industries, have contributed to declines in the real earnings of many young adults with no post-secondary schooling, and to an extension of the period of economic adolescence. This is particularly the case for males and race/ethnic minorities.

For many youth in poor families today, the journey from adolescence to young adulthood is a perilous one, containing a number of formidable barriers to making a successful transition to the adult economic and social world. Many poor teens do, however, manage to obtain the skills, schooling, and labor market experience needed to escape from the ranks of the poor by the time they reach their young adult years. But a combination of public and private actions on a variety of economic, educational, and social fronts is urgently needed to facilitate the transition out of poverty for an even greater number of today's adolescents.

MEASURING THE POOR ADOLESCENT POPULATION

Attempts to measure and describe the size and characteristics of the adolescent poverty population are dependent on definitions of both poverty and adolescence. The poverty income measures referred to in this chapter are those used by the Bureau of the Census in estimating the poverty population of the nation.[1] Defining the beginning and ending points of the adolescent stage of life is somewhat more difficult due to the diversity of views on which ages constitute adolescence, widespread recognition that the length of this stage is a variable one, and the close ties between adolescence and early adult life in the life cycle models of psychologists and other social scientists.[2] National commissions focusing on the transition from adolescence to adulthood have adopted a varying number of definitions. The Kettering Foundation's National Commission on Youth classified as "youth" those persons fourteen to twenty-one years of age, but noted that "the bridge of time between youth and adulthood has become a bridge too long."[3]

This chapter will primarily refer to the nation's thirteen-to-eighteen year olds as the adolescent population. It begins with an examination of trends in the size, demographic characteristics, and family living arrangements of the nation's adolescents, focusing on those adolescents living in poverty families. Following this is a presentation of data on key educational and employment experiences of poor adolescents as they move through their high school years. Their status and experiences are compared with and contrasted to those of similar-aged adolescents from higher income and higher socio-economic status backgrounds.

Finally, the chapter examines the experiences of poor youth as they attempt to move from adolescence to early adulthood, including the transition from high school to college and the labor market. Given the lengthier time needed by many youth in today's society for establishing a foothold in career labor markets, this analysis tracks the employment and earnings experiences of both poor teens and poor young adults through age twenty-four.[4] The use of twenty-four as an ending point is for expository purposes only. Many poor young adults remain confined in an "economic adolescence" stage at the end of this period.

TRENDS IN POVERTY AMONG THE NATION'S ADOLESCENTS

Progress in reducing problems of poverty among U.S. families and especially among families with children under eighteen came to a halt

CHART 1A

**Population and Poverty Status of
13 to 18 Year Olds, United States,
1974–1988
(Millions)**

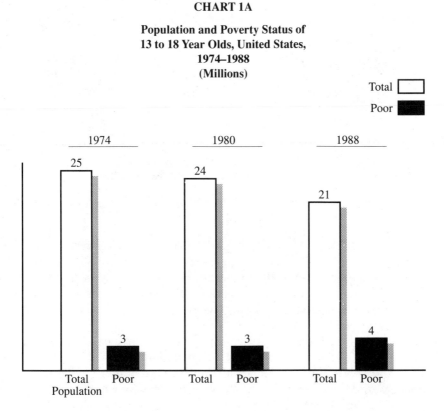

Source: March 1974, March 1980, and March 1988 CPS Public Use Tapes. Estimates generated by the authors.

CHART 1B

Race/Ethnicity of 13 to 18 Year Olds, United States, 1974–1988

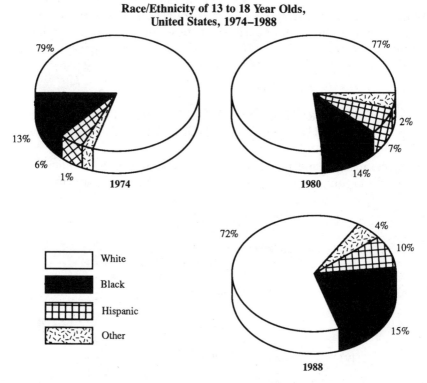

Source: March 1974, March 1980, and March 1988 CPS Public Use Tapes.
Estimates generated by the authors.
(Numbers do not add up to 100 due to rounding.)

in the early 1970s. Between 1959 and 1973, the family poverty rate fell by more than half, from 18.5 percent to 8.8 percent.[5] Since then, the rate of poverty among all families has tended to fluctuate between 9 and 12 percent, rising during periods of economic recession and declining somewhat as real family incomes rise in the wake of renewed economic growth.[6]

As a category, families with children have been particularly adversely affected by economic and social developments during the 1970s and 1980s. Between 1959 and 1969, the fraction of the nation's children under eighteen living in poor families declined from 27 percent to slightly under 14 percent and was still at 14.2 percent in 1973. Poverty among children has increased since then, reaching nearly 22 percent in 1983 and remaining close to 20 percent since

CHART 1C

**Family Living Arrangements,
13 to 18 Year Olds,
United States, 1974–1988**

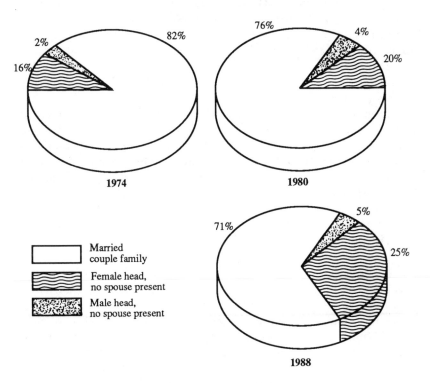

Source: March 1974, March 1980, and March 1988 CPS Public Use Tapes.
Estimates generated by the authors.
(Numbers do not add up to 100 due to rounding.)

1985, despite continued growth in employment and real family incomes for the population as a whole.

While little attention has been paid in recent years to the specific problems of adolescents, they too have become the victims of increasing family poverty. Trends in the numbers, demographic characteristics, family living arrangements, and poverty status of the nation's adolescent population (thirteen-to-eighteen) are summarized in Charts 1A, 1B, and 1C.[7]

The total number of adolescents in the United States declined over the 1974–1988 period, as the tail end of the "Baby Boom" generation passed through the teen-age years and was replaced in the adolescent age range by the members of the "Baby Bust" cohort. This shrinkage in the total population of adolescents was accompanied by a number of important changes in its race/ethnic composition and family living arrangements, and each of these changes have contributed to a sharp rise in the proportion of adolescents living in poverty.[8] In a span of about fifteen years, the relative number of American adolescents living in poor families increased from one-seventh to closer to one-fifth (Chart 1A). With the near-poor included, the fraction has risen to one-quarter.

A look at underlying demographic and family living arrangement factors associated with poverty status indicates why this has happened, and an analysis of the educational deficits increasingly related to adolescent poverty status suggests the potential for seriously increased adult poverty in future years, unless we succeed in changing the equation.

The Impact of Ethnicity and Family Status

In the mid-1970s, about one-fifth of the nation's adolescents were members of racial or ethnic minority groups—that is, were either nonwhite or Hispanic. By 1980, minorities' share of the adolescent population had increased to 23 percent, rising to over 28 percent by 1988. Minority teens, especially blacks and Hispanics, have typically exhibited poverty rates that are substantial multiples (three to five times) of white, non-Hispanic adolescent poverty rates (Chart 2A). The increase in the minority share of the nation's adolescent population, therefore—a trend that will continue throughout the remainder of this century—would be expected to place a greater share of adolescents at risk of being raised in a poverty family, especially if the future produces a lack of progress in reducing poverty among black and Hispanic families similar to that which occurred over the 1980s.

The continued high rate of dissolution of marriages, and a sustained rise in the proportion of births to unmarried mothers, have increased disproportionately the number of adolescents being raised by one-parent families[9], and thus in relatively low-income families. In the mid-1970s, about eight out of ten adolescents lived in married couple families; however, as the 1980s ended, this figure had decreased to about seven in ten.[10] This shift in family living arrangements has contributed to a rising trend of poverty among America's adolescents, in particular because of the substantially greater inci-

CHART 2A

Poverty Rates, 13 to 18 Year Olds, United States, 1974–1988 By Ethnic Group

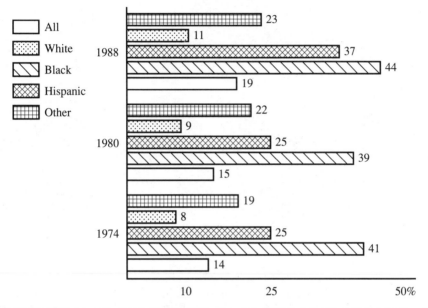

Source: March 1974, March 1980, and March 1988 CPS Public Use Tapes. Estimates generated by the authors.

dence of poverty among families headed by a woman with no spouse present. The poverty rate for adolescents living in families with an absent father was 47 percent in 1988. (Chart 2B). The incidence of poverty among adolescents in such families has been five to six times higher than that faced by teens living in married couple families.

As these changes in the composition and race/ethnic background of the U.S. teen population occurred, the size of the group over all declined. The estimated aggregate number of adolescents *declined* by nearly 4 million between 1974 and 1988, but the number of adolescents living in poor families *increased* by one-half million, rising to 3.9 million in 1988.[11] The rise in the incidence of poverty affected adolescents in each major racial and ethnic group, but large race/ethnic differences in the incidence of poverty among adolescents continue to prevail, with Hispanics having suffered the largest absolute and relative increases in poverty during this period. In March

CHART 2B

**Poverty Rates of 13 to 18 Year Olds,
By Family Living Arrangement, 1988**

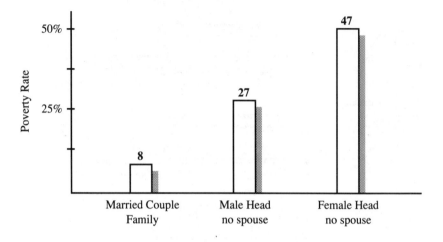

Source: March 1988 CPS Public Use Tape.

1988, nearly four of every nine black adolescents and three of every eight Hispanic teens were poor, compared with one of every nine white, non-Hispanic adolescents (Chart 2A).

The adverse consequences of living in a poverty family would be less severe for adolescents if their family's poverty status were a highly transitory one. Recent national evidence on exit rates out of poverty reveals, however, that families with children under eighteen have high rates of long-duration poverty.[12] Findings from the federal government's Survey of Income and Program Participation indicate, for example, that nearly 80 percent of those under eighteen who were living in poor families in 1984 were also members of poor families in 1985—almost 90 percent if near-poor families are included.[13]

The trend in the family living arrangements of poor adolescents over the past fifteen years does not bode well for the future. The proportion of adolescent poor living in a family headed by a woman with no husband present has been rising. It went up from 51 percent in 1974 to 62 percent in 1988 (Chart 3). In addition, an increasing proportion reside in families with only the father present in the home. Poor black adolescents are at greatest risk of the longer-term family poverty associated with single-parent status. Eighty-two per-

CHART 3

Distribution of Poor Teens in U.S.
By Family Type, March 1988

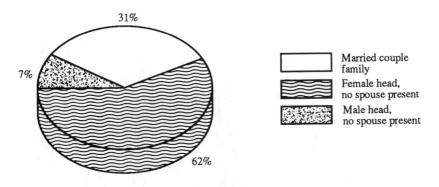

Source: March 1974, March 1980, and March 1988 CPS Public Use Tapes.
Estimates generated by the authors.

cent were living in single-parent families in 1988, versus 53 percent and 60 percent of the Hispanic and white poor adolescents, respectively.

Geographic Variations in Adolescent Poverty

While adolescent poverty problems vary in intensity by geographic location across the nation, they are not confined to any one region or to large central cities or depressed rural areas. During March 1988, the proportion of children thirteen to eighteen living in poverty families ranged from 15 percent in the Northeast to 22 percent in the South (Chart 4A). Further, the incidence of poverty among the nation's adolescents rose in each major geographic region between 1974 and 1988, but South/non-South poverty differentials narrowed considerably between 1974 and 1988, due to increases in adolescent poverty in the non-South regions.

Adolescents living in the nation's central cities continue to face the most severe poverty problems; however, poverty rates among adolescents have increased in metropolitan areas outside of the central city and in non-metropolitan areas as well (Chart 4B).[14] During March 1988, over 28 percent of the adolescents in the nation's central cities

CHART 4A

**Poverty Rates of 13 to 18 Year Olds,
By Geographic Region, 1974–1988**

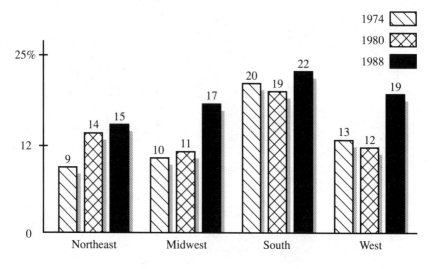

CHART 4B

**Poverty Rates of 13 to 18 Year Olds,
By Metro and Non-Metro Areas,
1974–1988**

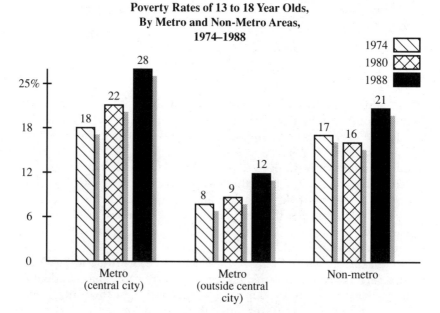

Source: March 1974, March 1980, and March 1988 CPS Public Use Tapes.

were living in poor families, compared to 21 percent of those in non-metropolitan areas and 12 percent of those in metropolitan areas outside of the central cities. While the national media tend to focus public attention on those poor children who live in the nation's central cities, less than 40 percent of all poor adolescents in March 1988 were living in a central city, and the nation's twenty largest central cities contained only one of every five poor adolescents. Poor adolescents living in large central cities are, however, at greater risk of persistent poverty, because they live somewhat more predominantly in families with only the mother present in the home. During March 1988, nearly 70 percent of poor teens in the nation's twenty largest central cities were living in one-parent, female-headed families, versus slightly under 60 percent of poor adolescents living elsewhere.

The Pre-Teen Population

The U.S. adolescent population living in poverty will almost surely increase over the 1990s. Recent trends in race/ethnic group composition and family living arrangements are likely to continue throughout the remainder of the century and, in the absence of any fundamental shift in the growth path of real family incomes, these trends inevitably will increase adolescent poverty rates. An examination of the characteristics of the population of children seven to twelve in 1988 (the age cohort that will be thirteen to eighteen in the middle of the 1990s) reveals that 30 percent were members of race/ethnic minority groups, and 26 percent were living in single-parent families (Charts 5A and 5B).

Approximately one-fifth of these pre-teens were living in poor families (Chart 5C): and, as is the case with their slightly older adolescent counterparts, black and Hispanic pre-teens were considerably more likely than white pre-teens to be members of poor families. Because the large numbers of women in the baby boom cohort produced a high level of births in the late 1970s and early 1980s, the absolute number of teenagers will begin to rise in the middle part of the 1990s.[15] Thus, failure to reduce the high incidence of poverty among families with young children today will lead to an even greater absolute number of poor adolescents in the nation throughout the remainder of this century.

Adolescent Childbearing

Over the past decade, there has been increased attention by public policymakers, the media, researchers, and children's advocacy organ-

CHART 5A

**Distribution of U.S. Pre-Teens,
By Race/Ethnic Group
1988**

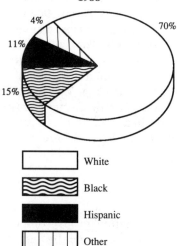

White

Black

Hispanic

Other

CHART 5B

**Distribution of U.S. Pre-Teens
By Family Living Arrangements
1988**

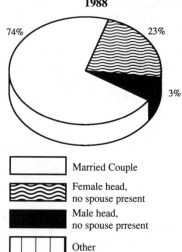

Married Couple

Female head,
no spouse present

Male head,
no spouse prresent

Other

Source: March 1988 CPS Public Use Tape.

CHART 5C

**Poverty Rates of U.S. Pre-Teens,
1988**

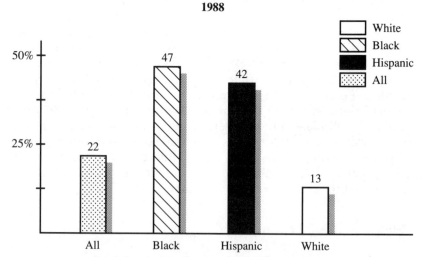

White

Black

Hispanic

All

Source: March 1988 CPS Public Use Tape.

izations to the issue of teenage childbearing, despite the fact that the total number of births to teenage mothers continued to decline throughout the 1980s. The concern results from an understanding that teen pregnancy is associated with greater health problems encountered by the children born to teenage mothers, greater educational deficits experienced by women who bear children in their early adolescent years, high rates of poverty among never-married women who became mothers in their teenage years, and the public costs of the economic dependency of women who give birth as children.[16]

The total number of live births to teenage mothers in the U.S. fell fairly steadily over the 1970–88 period, producing fewer than 490,000 such births per year since 1985 (Chart 6A). The decline in the number of births to teen mothers over the past decade, however, has been due primarily to a reduction in the size of the nation's teenage population rather than to any sustained drop in the birthrate among teens. During 1988, the estimated birthrate among 15–19 year olds was 54 per 1,000, slightly above the rate of 52 per 1,000 similar-aged women in 1978 (Chart 6B).

Further, while the total number of births to teens has fallen over time, the share of these births to unmarried women has been rising over time. By 1988, nearly two of every three births to teens occurred outside of marriage, a more than doubling of the fraction of births to unmarried teen mothers in 1970 (Chart 6C). Among black teen mothers, 91 of every 100 births in 1987 took place out of wedlock. (Chart 7).

CHART 6A

**Number of Live Births
to U.S. Teens
Selected Years, 1970–1988**

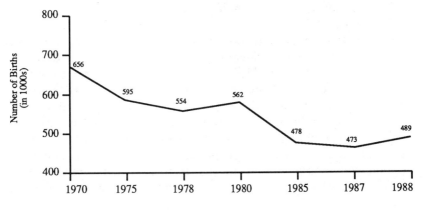

CHART 6B

**U.S. Births Per 1,000 Women
15 to 19 Year Olds
Selected Years, 1970–1988**

Source: (i) U.S. Department of Commerce, Bureau of the Census,
        Statistical Abstract of the U.S., 1988, "Table 83," p. 60.
       (ii) Kristin Moore, Child Trends, "Facts At A Glance," 1989.
      (iii) U.S. National Center for Health Statistics. Data provided by
        the authors.

It should be noted that growth in the fraction of births taking place outside of marriage has not been confined to the nation's teenagers. Among 20–24 year old women, the percent of births to unmarried mothers more than tripled between 1970 and 1987, rising from 9 percent to nearly 31 percent (Chart 8A). As recently as 1975, a slight majority (52%) of all out-of-wedlock births were accounted for by teenagers (Chart 8B). By 1987, teens were responsible for less than one-third of all births to unmarried women. The rising fraction of births among teens and young adults taking place outside of marriage has had a major impact upon the living arrangements and poverty status of children in the nation's youngest families and subfamilies, contributing to the overall increase in family poverty noted above.[17]

The incidence of childbearing among adolescents varies quite widely by demographic and socioeconomic subgroup, with minority teens, low-income teens, school dropouts, and those with weak basic academic skills being considerably more likely to bear a child during their teenage years.[18]

The short-term economic prospects for many teenage mothers, especially those giving birth to their children outside of wedlock, are admittedly quite bleak. These women and their children are not, however, doomed to a life of poverty or dependency. A longitudinal study of the longer-term life experiences of a sample of Baltimore women who became mothers in their teenage years has revealed that many of them were able to avoid becoming trapped in a world of

CHART 6C

**Percentage of Out-of-Wedlock Births
to Teenage Women in U.S.
Selected Years, 1970–1988**

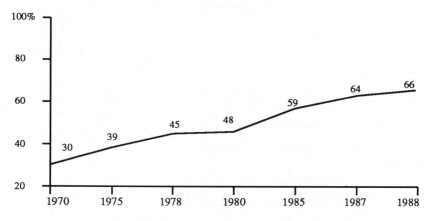

**U.S. Births Per 1,000 Women Under 15
Selected Years, 1970–1988**

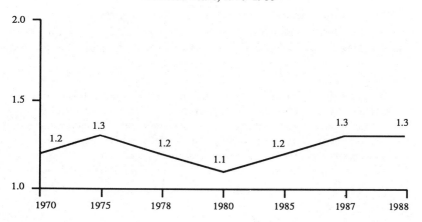

Source: (i) U.S. Department of Commerce, Bureau of the Census, Statistical Abstract of the U.S., 1988, "Table 83," p. 60.
(ii) Kristin Moore, Child Trends, "Facts At A Glance," 1989.
(iii) U.S. National Center for Health Statistics. Data provided by the authors.

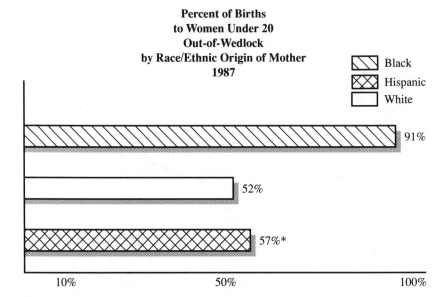

CHART 7

Percent of Births
to Women Under 20
Out-of-Wedlock
by Race/Ethnic Origin of Mother
1987

Black
Hispanic
White

91%

52%

57%*

10%   50%   100%

Source: Vital Statistics Program.

Note: Based on Hispanic birth data reported by 23 states and the District of
         Columbia.

poverty or dependence on welfare for their economic livelihood.[19] There were steps, including further education, stable employment, and marriage, that significantly improved their chances of escaping from poverty. As the authors of the study noted:

> "There are life courses characterized by welfare dependency, non-marriage, low education and high fertility. . . . Those whose life course takes on such a trajectory are likely to remain on this path. But if individuals alter this trajectory by getting a stable job, entering a stable marriage, acquiring educational credentials or curtailing subsequent fertility, then they are no more likely than others to fall back within this trajectory."[20]

EDUCATION AND EMPLOYMENT: THE CRITICAL ISSUES

In a recent study tracking the poverty status of a sample of individuals from their adolescent years into young adulthood, it was found that

CHART 8A

**Percent of U.S. Births Out-of-Wedlock
to Women 20 to 24 Years Old
Selected Years, 1970–1988**

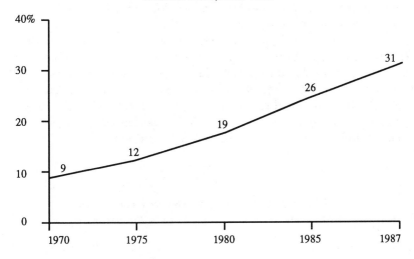

CHART 8B

**Percent of U.S. Births to
Non-Married Teenage Women
Selected Years, 1970–1988**

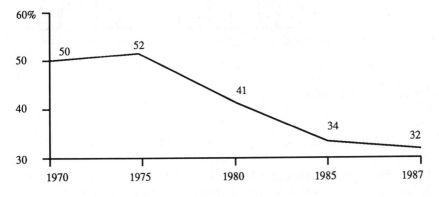

Source: U.S. National Center for Health Statistics. Data provided to
authors.

about 35 percent of those youth (fourteen to seventeen) who were poor in 1979 were also poor seven years later in 1986.[21] This in itself is an extremely important finding, because it means that there *are* high escape rates from poverty for adolescents over time. Yet it remains true that poor adolescents are four times as likely as non-poor adolescents to be poor as young adults.

One critical factor influencing escape rates from poverty is educational attainment. Both for poor adolescents and for non-poor adolescents, the likelihood of poverty in the young adult years is strongly associated with poor performance in, and failure to complete, high school (Chart 9). Another factor, one that pertains especially to poor young people, is inadequate "bonding experiences" with the labor market during the early school-to-work transition years.

CHART 9

Percent of 21 to 24 Year Olds Who Were Poor in 1985
By Educational Attainment and Family Poverty Status

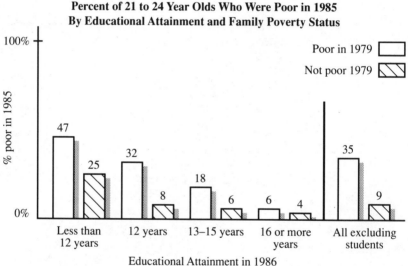

Source: NLS Public Use Tape, 1979–1986 Interviews.

Income and Education

During the early years of adolescence (thirteen to fifteen), nearly all teenagers are enrolled in school, though the attendance behavior of some youth is sufficiently sporadic to classify them as truants. As adolescents proceed through their teenage years, together with their parents and school staff they make important choices in relation to the types of educational programs and courses in which to enroll, the amount of time to devote to school studies and homework, whether to remain in high school through graduation, whether to attend college after obtaining a high school diploma or a GED certificate, and then which schools to attend. Given important changes in the industrial, occupational, and wage structure of the American economy that have occurred over the past couple of decades, these decisions about the amount, type, and quality of schooling to obtain now have more critical long-term implications for youths' economic and social well-being.[22]

Over a period of less than fifteen years—from 1973 to 1986—the real income value of a high school diploma for young men in the U.S. declined dramatically. In 1973, the median annual income of thirty-year-old males who had completed four years of college was about 15 percent higher than the median annual income of those who only had completed high school. That is a noticeable but not astonishing difference. By 1986, however, the data indicate that this gap had widened to 50 percent.[23] The larger gap does not reflect a sudden rise in the value of a college education. In fact, the numbers suggest that the annual income value of a college degree, in real dollars, slipped a little over the period. The earnings associated with a high school diploma, though, slipped a great deal—from just about $25,000 per year in 1972, to about $18,000 per year in 1986.

Thus there now are fewer opportunities to earn even a moderate income in the U.S. economy for an individual who does not do well in school. And poor teenagers are far less likely to do well in school than non-poor teenagers. The former have weaker basic skills as they enter the teen years, and they therefore predictably tend to fall behind as their junior high and high school years go by. They are often tracked out of college preparatory programs, their educational aspirations lag behind those of their better-off peers, and their educational expectations are lower still. And—again, no surprise— poorer adolescents are much more likely to drop out of high school before graduation.

Basic Academic Skills

Many poor youth are at a serious disadvantage with respect to academic achievement and performance. On average, adolescents from poor families tend to have far weaker basic academic proficiency. An examination of the median test scores of fifteen-to-sixteen and seventeen-to-eighteen year olds on the Armed Forces Qualification Test (AFQT) administered to a nationally representative sample of youth during the summer of 1980 revealed quite clearly the magnitude of these deficits.[24] While these data are now a decade old, they remain one of the best available standardized nationwide indicators of the nature of a problem that is usually measured only at the local level. The AFQT test measures proficiencies in the following basic academic areas: word knowledge, paragraph comprehension, arithmetic reasoning, and numerical operations.[25] The on-going National Assessment of Educational Progress (NAEP) measures many of these proficiencies, but only for in-school teens and provides no poverty breakouts.

In 1980, the median AFQT test scores of poor fifteen-to-sixteen and seventeen-to-eighteen year olds were considerably below those of their non-poor counterparts (Chart 10). The median AFQT test score of a fifteen-to-sixteen year old living in a poverty family fell at the 18th percentile of the test score distribution. Similar findings apply to the test performance of poor seventeen-to-eighteen year olds.[26]

CHART 10

U.S. Percentile Rankings of 15 to 16
and 17 to 18 Year Olds on
AFQT Test Scores, 1980

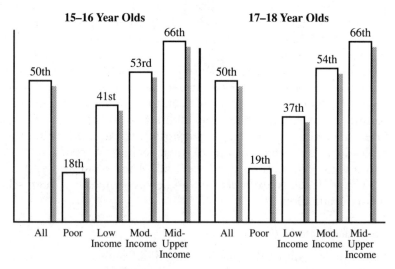

Source: NLS Public Use Tape, 1979–1986 Interviews.

Note: Poor persons are those living below the federally-established poverty threshold, which in 1980 was an income of $8,385 per year for a family of four.

Poor blacks and Hispanics were even more concentrated in the bottom fifth of the distribution, placing them at a substantial competitive disadvantage in school and in the labor market. The 1982 achievement test scores of high school seniors participating in the High School and Beyond Longitudinal Study also showed considerable variation in test score performance related to family socioeconomic status.[27]

The basic academic skill deficits of many poor adolescents affects their school behavior adversely as well. Youth with better basic academic skills spend more time in academic courses, take more of them, and invest more time in homework.[28] Basic academic proficiencies of adolescents are an important determinant of school performance overall. Students with weak academic skills more frequently fail courses and are held back in grade. An analysis of the AFQT test scores of fourteen-to-eighteen year old adolescents enrolled in school in 1979 revealed that those students two or more years behind modal grade for their age group had mean test scores that were 1.0 to 1.5 standard deviations below those of their peers at or above modal grade.[29]

High School Programs

The high school experiences of poor adolescents differ from those of middle class and upper middle class youth in a number of substantive respects, beyond the single fact of academic achievement. Among the key differences are the characteristics of the schools which they attend, the socioeconomic backgrounds of their fellow students, the types of school programs in which they enroll, and the academic orientations of the courses that they take.[30] During their early high school years, adolescents from poor families tend to be over-represented in "general" school programs (62%) and under-represented in college preparatory programs (19%), relative to their counterparts from more affluent family backgrounds. The concentration of poor adolescents in general programs holds true for blacks, Hispanics, and whites (Chart 11A).

As students move through their high school years, more of them shift out of general courses and into vocational and commercial programs. During 1979, a slight majority (52%) of high school juniors and seniors were enrolled in general academic programs, 31 percent were in college preparatory programs, and the remaining 17 percent were in vocational or commercial programs (Chart 11B). Juniors and seniors from poor families (62%) were most likely to be enrolled in general academic programs and least likely to be participating in a

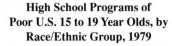

CHART 11A

High School Programs of
Poor U.S. 15 to 19 Year Olds, by
Race/Ethnic Group, 1979

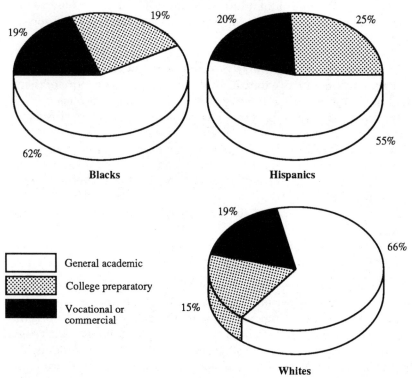

Source: 1979 NLS Public Use Tape.

college preparatory program. Contrary to conventional wisdom, though, poor adolescents are *not* more likely to be found in vocational or commercial courses.

The under-representation of poor high school students in college preparatory programs has some not-so-obvious consequences for future academic achievement and ultimate educational attainment. Enrollment in a college preparatory program tends to have independent positive impacts on the basic academic proficiencies of students, their educational aspirations, their likelihood of leaving high school with a diploma, and their college attendance behavior after high school.[31]

CHART 11B

High School Programs for 15 to 19 Year Olds
by Family Income, 1979

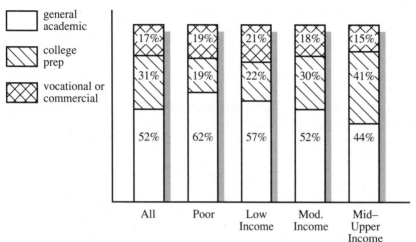

Source: 1979 NLS Public Use Tape.

Educational Aspirations and Expectations

The educational aspirations of adolescents are an important variable in their own right, and they have been found to influence independently the dropout behavior of high school students, the return to school rates of former dropouts, and the college attendance behavior of high school graduates.[32] The educational aspirations and expectations of adolescents are not randomly distributed across the youth population, but instead vary systematically with parents' educational backgrounds, family income, school experiences, and academic achievement. Adolescents whose parents have completed some post-secondary schooling, who live in higher income families, who are enrolled in college preparatory programs, and who have stronger basic academic skills have significantly higher educational expectations.[33]

The educational aspirations and expectations of fourteen-to-seventeen year old adolescents at the time of the 1979 NLS interview are summarized in Charts 12A and B, together with summary measures of the degree of congruence between their aspirations and their expectations. In general, educational aspirations of these adolescents were quite high. Nearly 99 percent of them wanted to obtain a high school diploma, 63 percent wished to complete some post-secondary schooling, and 50 percent wanted to obtain a four-year college degree. The overwhelming majority (96%) of adolescents residing in poor families wanted to obtain a high school diploma, and nearly one-third aspired to be college graduates. Not surprisingly, though, the proportion of these fourteen-to-seventeen year old adolescents aspiring to be college graduates varied with their family's relative income position. Nearly five of eight adolescents living in families with moderate to upper high incomes wanted to obtain a four-year degree. This ratio was nearly twice as high as that of poor adolescents (Chart 12A).

The educational expectations of adolescents in all family income categories tended to fall somewhat short of aspirations; however, congruence between educational desires and expectations was weakest

CHART 12A

**Education Desired by U.S. 14 to 17 Year Olds
By Family Income, 1979**

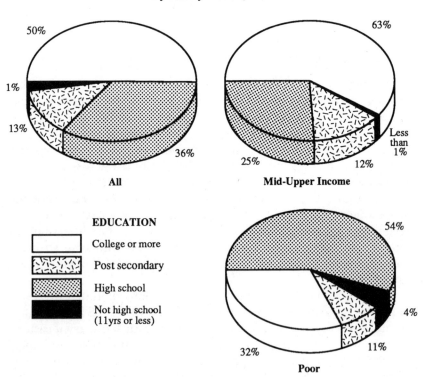

Source: 1979 National Longitudinal Survey Public Use Tape.

for youth from poor families. While 96 percent of poor adolescents said they wanted to complete high school, only 88 percent expected to obtain a high school diploma and, although 32 percent aspired to graduate from college, only 21 percent expected to complete four years of college (Charts 12A and B).

The educational expectations of the 1980 high school seniors participating in the High School and Beyond study also varied widely by family socioeconomic status.[34] Fifty-eight percent of the seniors expected to complete two or more years of college and 46 percent expected to obtain a four-year college degree.[35] Seniors from low SES backgrounds were least likely to expect to graduate from a four-year college or university. Only 26 percent of low SES students expected

CHART 12B

**Education Expected by U.S. 14 to 17 Year Olds
by Family Income, 1979**

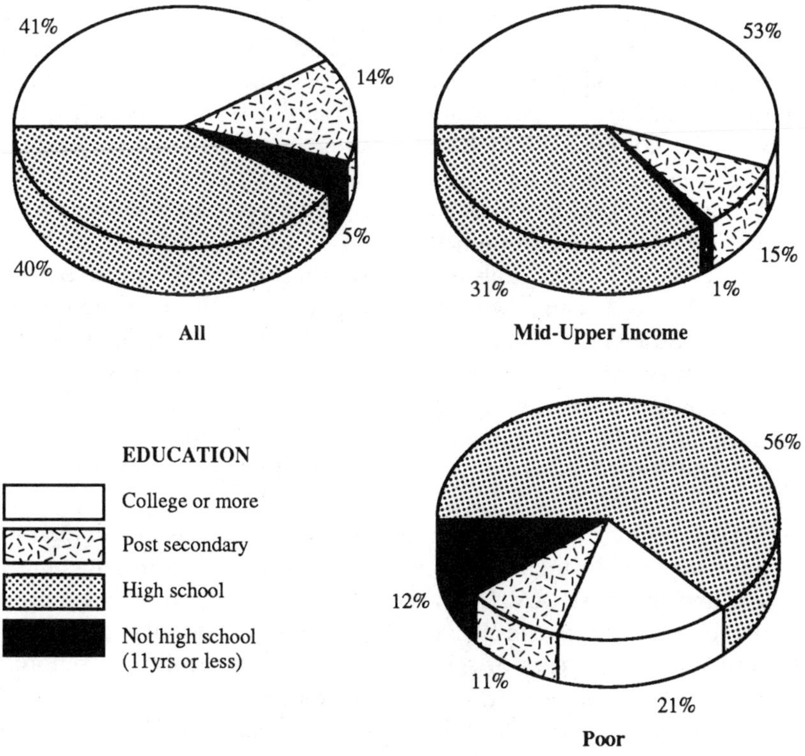

All

Mid-Upper Income

EDUCATION

College or more

Post secondary

High school

Not high school
(11yrs or less)

Poor

Source: 1979 National Longitudinal Survey Public Use Tape.

to complete four years of college versus 41 percent of those in the middle SES categories and 76 percent of those in the high SES category—that is, the top quantile of the SES distribution. As was indicated by findings from the 1979 NLS survey, educational expectations were strongly associated with academic achievement for these seniors.[36]

School Dropout Behavior

Given their deficient basic academic skills, their greater tendency to be two or more years of school behind their age group, their lower educational expectations, and their weaker "social capital" support systems, one would expect poor adolescents to be at far greater risk of dropping out of school before graduation.[37] School dropout rates of fourteen-to-fifteen year old students over a two-year period clearly reveal strong associations between dropout behavior and the family income backgrounds and basic academic skills of young adolescents.

Approximately one of every ten students fourteen-to-fifteen years old in 1979 would leave school without a diploma by 1981. Those adolescents living in poverty families had the highest incidence of dropping out. Slightly more than 20 percent of adolescents from poor families left school between 1979 and 1981, versus 12 percent of those in families with moderate income and only 6 percent of those living in families with mid-upper income (Chart 13A).

School dropout rates also are strongly associated with lack of academic skills. Nearly one-fifth of those fourteen-to-fifteen year old adolescents with basic skills test scores (on the AFQT) in the bottom quintile had left school, versus only 8 percent of those in the middle quintile and less than 3 percent of those in the top quintile of the test score distribution (Chart 13B). Among poor adolescents, dropout rates typically remain well above those of more affluent youth until the top academic skill categories are reached. Unfortunately, only a small fraction of poor adolescents reach the top categories of the skills distribution.[38]

More recent evidence on the dropout problems of sixteen-to-nineteen year old teens by race/ethnic group and family income is presented in Chart 14A. In March 1988, 10 percent of all sixteen-to-nineteen year olds in the civilian non-institutional population had not completed twelve years of school and were not enrolled in school.[39] The proportion of teens who had left school before graduation varied markedly by family income background. Nearly one-fourth of the poor were school dropouts, while only four percent of those living in middle to upper-income families (the top 50% of families in terms of

CHART 13A

Percent of U.S. 14 to 15 Year Old Students Who Dropped Out of School Within Two Years, By Family Income, 1979–1981

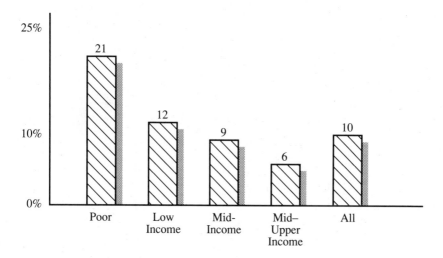

CHART 13B

Percent of U.S. 14 to 15 Year Old Students Who Dropped Out of School Within Two Years, By Position in the Basic Skills Test Distribution, 1979–1981

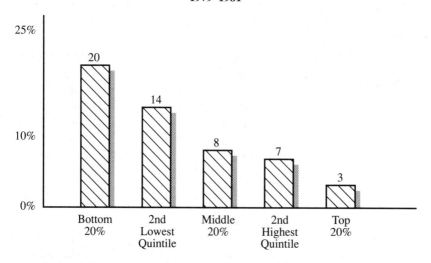

Source: NLS public use tapes, 1979 to 1981 interview rounds.

CHART 14A

Incidence of School Dropout Problems Among U.S. 16 to 19 Year Olds,
By Race/Ethnic Group and Family Income, 1988

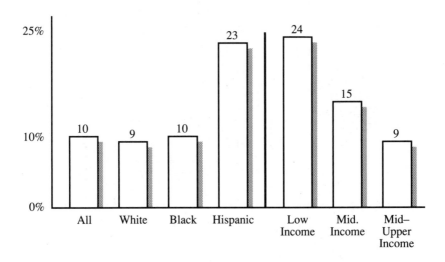

income) had left school before receiving a diploma. Among the poor, Hispanic teens (33%) were the most likely to have dropped out, and they tended to leave school with the fewest years of schooling completed (Chart 14B).

Poor youth who drop out of school before graduation tend to have extremely limited quantitative and verbal skills as well as less exposure to the core of knowledge contained in the high school curriculum, a fact that will place them at a substantial disadvantage in their young adult years.[40] Given that academic achievement generally rises with the number of years of schooling completed, pre-existing achievement gaps between dropouts and the in-school adolescent population tend to become even wider gaps over time.[41] While many school dropouts do eventually return to school and acquire a diploma or a GED certificate, the likelihood of doing so is positively associated with the academic proficiencies they had before dropping out.[42]

Given their relatively lower academic proficiencies, poor dropouts are therefore less likely than their counterparts from higher family income backgrounds to complete their high school educations as young adults. As a consequence, poor young adults tend to appear in very large concentrations in the bottom 20 percent of the distribution of literacy proficiencies, and poor young adult dropouts typically fall

CHART 14B

Incidence of School Dropout Problems Among Poor U.S. 16 to 19 Year Olds, By Race/Ethnic Group, 1988

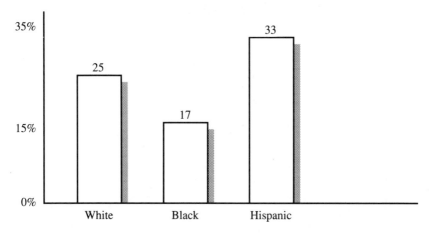

Source: March 1988 CPS Public Use Tape.

within the bottom 10 percent of the literacy distribution for all young adults throughout the nation.[43]

Research over many years has shown consistently that the basic academic proficiencies of teens and young adults are critically influenced by the educational attainment of their parents.[44] The limited educational attainment of the current generation of poor youth thus is bound to have adverse inter-generational consequences for the educational attainment of their children.

The Transition from High School to College

During the 1980s, a rising fraction of each year's high school graduating class has been enrolling in college in the fall immediately following graduation.[45] In the fall of 1988, nearly 60 percent of the cohort of 1988 high school graduates was enrolled in college, a record-high rate of college attendance.[46] Studies of the college enrollment behavior of America's high school graduates have found that the academic performance and aptitudes of high school students and their family socio-economic backgrounds critically influence their college attendance decisions.[47]

The early college attendance behavior of seventeen-to-twenty year old high school graduates from the Class of 1979 is portrayed in Charts 15A and B. Approximately 47 percent of the respondents

CHART 15A

**Percent of Graduating High School Seniors 17 to 20 Years Old,
Who Enrolled in College, By Family Income, 1979**

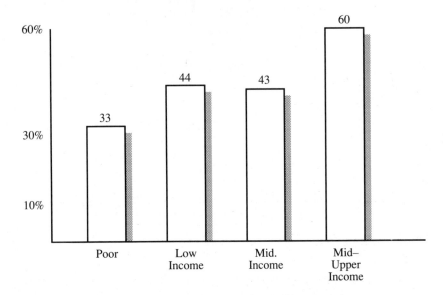

were enrolled in a post-secondary educational program in the winter/ spring of the year immediately following graduation. College attendance rates varied considerably by the family income position of these students during the senior year, as well as their ranking in the AFQT test score distribution for juniors and seniors.[48] Only one-third of the graduates from poor families were attending college, while 42 to 44 percent of those with moderate family incomes were doing so, as were nearly 60 percent of the graduates with high family incomes (Chart 15A).

The percent of graduates attending college also was strongly associated with their relative position in the basic academic skills distribution which, as noted, is itself associated with family income. Only one of seven graduates with AFQT test scores in the bottom quintile were attending college, versus 35 percent of those in the middle quintile and 78 percent of those in the top quintile of the test score distribution (Chart 15B).

An analysis of the college attendance behavior of 1979 high school seniors revealed that youth from poverty families were 42 percent less likely than their non-poor counterparts to attend college in the following year.[49] The findings of this study assessing the factors

CHART 15B

**Percent of Graduating High School Seniors 17 to 20 Years Old,
Who Enrolled in College, By Position in Basic Skills Test Distribution,
1979**

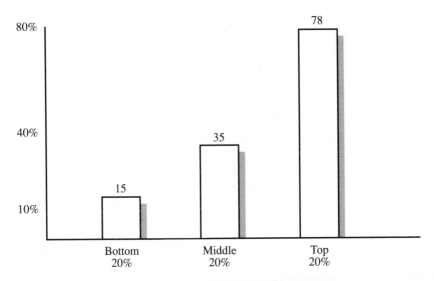

Source: 1979 and 1980 NLS surveys of Youth Labor Market Experience.

influencing college attendance indicated that poverty *per se* was not the critical factor.[50] Instead, the personal and parental background traits frequently associated with a poverty family environment were the decisive factors. Students with weak academic proficiencies, two or more years behind modal grade, not enrolled in a college preparatory program, and with parents lacking any post-secondary schooling were significantly less likely to attend college. It is thus the schooling experiences of poor high school students and their far weaker academic proficiencies, both associated with but not equivalent to poverty, that place them at a serious disadvantage relative to their more affluent counterparts in relation to college attendance.

Findings of the 1982 and 1984 follow-up surveys of the High School and Beyond longitudinal tracking of the Class of 1980 provide more recent information on the post-secondary educational and training experiences of youth from different socio-economic backgrounds.[51] During the first twenty to twenty-one months following graduation, approximately 63 percent of the seniors from the Class of 1980 had entered post-secondary education or training programs (Chart 16A).[52] Thirty-five percent of these seniors went on to enroll

CHART 16A

Post-Secondary Enrollment Rates of U.S. High School Seniors, 1980

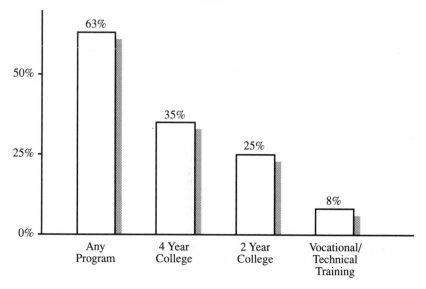

in a four-year college, 25 percent attended a two-year college, and 8 percent enrolled in a vocational/technical training program.

High school graduates from low SES backgrounds were least likely (46%) to have attended a post-secondary program, and they were substantially under-represented in four-year colleges and universities. Less than one in five graduates from low SES backgrounds attended a four-year college, versus one-third of those from middle SES backgrounds and 61 percent of those from high SES backgrounds (Chart 16B). Attrition problems also appear to have been more severe among low SES students attending two- and four-year colleges throughout this period. By February 1982, 15 percent of the students from low SES backgrounds attending four-year colleges had withdrawn, as had 31 percent of those attending two-year colleges.[53] The comparable ratios for high SES students were 7 percent and 20 percent, respectively.

Substantial differences among the post-secondary education and training enrollment rates of socioeconomic subgroups also prevailed at the time of the spring 1984 follow-up survey.[54] These large gaps in college attendance rates by socio-economic sub-group are likely to lead to severe long-term earnings inequality, given increasingly substantial differences in earnings capacity associated with years of formal schooling in the young adult years.[55]

CHART 16B

**Four-Year College Attendance Rates of High School Seniors
by Family Socio-Economic Status, 1980**

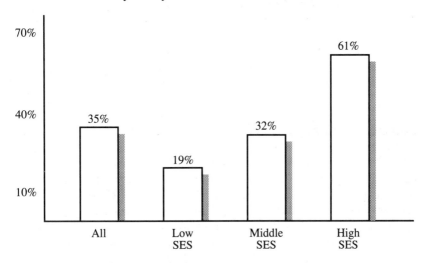

Source: National Center for Education Statistics, *Two Years After High School:
A Capsule Description of 1980 Seniors.*

The continued limited participation of youth from poor families and low SES backgrounds in the nation's post-secondary educational system, especially four-year colleges and universities, thus raises important questions about the role of higher education participation in reinforcing existing social and economic inequalities in American society. Large gaps in college enrollment and completion rates are particularly troublesome in an economic era where earnings differentials by formal schooling have widened. A *Washington Post* article on "Class, Color, and College," cited the following passage from the 1947 report of the President's Commission on Higher Education, as particularly relevant today:

> "If the ladder of educational opportunity rises high at the doors of some youth and scarcely rises at all at the doors of others, while at the same time formal education is made a prerequisite to occupational and social advance, then education may become the means, not of eliminating race and class distinctions, but of deepening and solidifying them."[56]

Apprenticeship, Training and Transition to the Labor Force

While poor high school graduates and those from low SES backgrounds are considerably less likely than their non-poor counterparts to enroll in college following graduation, they also do not appear to be any more successful in gaining access to apprenticeship training programs in the first four years following graduation from high school. A four-year follow-up survey of a nationally representative sample of 1980 high school graduates discovered that only one percent of the respondents from low socio-economic backgrounds were participating in an apprenticeship program four years after graduation, even though they were more likely to be working than their counterparts from higher socio-economic backgrounds.[57]

Education and Employment

The fact of growing up in a poor family—one where a parent or parents may well have weak labor force attachments, or none at all—has future employment consequences for the poor adolescent that are separate from, although related to, the adverse effects of poverty on school performance that lead to low college attendance. Poor young people still in high school are less likely to have the entry-level, part-time jobs that begin to generate both income and work experience. At post-high school ages, these young people are less likely to be either employed full-time or to be in post-secondary education or training programs. During this period, limited labor force experience combined with weak skills begins to place many poor young adolescents on a path that leads to a future of joblessness and low income. For boys, this path may lead also to drug and alcohol abuse, or antisocial behavior, or both. For girls, it may mean drug or alcohol addiction, early pregnancy, and a life of welfare dependency.

In-School Employment Experiences

Many adolescents in the United States become active participants in the labor market well before graduation from high school. The fraction of youth holding jobs rises fairly steadily during the teenage years, beginning with age fourteen.[58]

The nature of the jobs held by teens during the high school years and the intensity of their employment commitment also change as they age; however, most of the jobs they acquire during these years are relatively unskilled and frequently require limited formal schooling.[59] Adolescents from poor families, however, are the least likely to obtain employment at each stage, and poor minority teens are at greatest risk of joblessness.

Fairly large employment gaps between poor adolescents and their more affluent counterparts arise at ages fourteen to fifteen. Findings from the 1979 National Longitudinal Survey of Youth Labor Market Experience revealed that approximately one of four fourteen-to-fifteen year olds were employed at the time of the first-round interviews (Chart 17).[60] The employment rates of these young adolescents varied considerably by family income and race/ethnic group. Only one in six of the youth from poor families held jobs, while nearly three in ten youth from families with upper incomes did so. Among the poor, whites were considerably more likely than Hispanics or blacks to be employed (26% vs. 16% and 8%, respectively).

The vast majority of the jobs held by these fourteen-to-fifteen year olds involved a limited number of hours of work per week. The median was eight hours. Roughly 63 percent of the employed worked fewer than ten hours, although employed blacks and Hispanics worked more hours per week than whites.[61] Many of the jobs held by teens paid wages below the federal minimum, because they were often in private households or in small retail or private service firms not covered by the provisions of the federal minimum wage law.[62]

While these jobs were highly concentrated (80%) in a limited number of low-skill occupations (private household workers, other service occupations, sales, and laborers), they did provide adolescents an opportunity to acquire general work habits, assume some responsibility, and earn an income to finance personal and family consumption. Many middle and upper middle-income families encourage such work effort by their children, and adolescents from such families are often better positioned economically and socially to obtain access to jobs. Those fourteen-to-fifteen year-old adolescents who worked in 1979 were significantly more likely to be employed two years later, although these very early work experiences did not seem to affect their hourly wages.[63] Their early labor market attachment did not appear to have any adverse impacts on school enrollment two years later.

Findings on the employment experiences of fourteen-to-fifteen year olds from the Current Population Survey have been found to significantly under-estimate job attachment among these young adolescents (Chart 17).[64] The March CPS findings for the 1980s, though, typically reveal quite similar employment patterns. Fourteen and fifteen year olds from poor families are far less likely than those from more affluent backgrounds to be employed, and poor minority youth are the least likely to hold jobs. More recent findings, for March 1987 and March 1988, portray a similar situation. Young adolescents from poor families are only one-half to one-fourth as likely to be employed as similar-aged youth living in families with incomes three times the

CHART 17

**Employment/Population Ratios of U.S. 14 to 15 Year Olds By
Race/Ethnic Group and Family Income, 1979 and 1988**

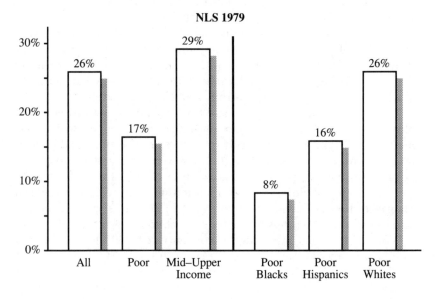

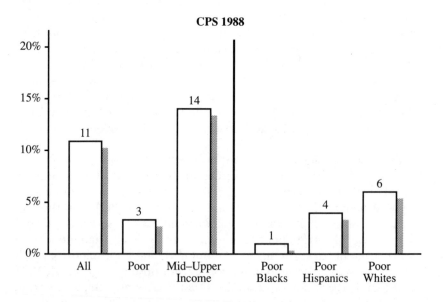

Source: CPS Tapes, March 1979, 1987, 1988; NLS, 1979.

poverty line. Only a tiny fraction of poor black and Hispanic youth (1% to 4%) get jobs during these early adolescent years.

While the employment rates of all major subgroups of students rise throughout the high school years, large gaps between the employment rates of the poor and the non-poor persist. Findings of the 1979 and 1980 NLS interviews with respect to sixteen-to-nineteen year old high school students revealed that 46 percent were employed at the time of both interviews (Chart 18A).[65] Only 28 percent of poor high school students were employed at the time of these interviews, in comparison with 53 percent of those students living in families with mid-to-upper-incomes. Among poor adolescents, blacks again were the least likely to be employed, followed by Hispanics and whites. These rather large employment gaps would have been even higher in the absence of a comprehensive set of job creation programs for poor and minority youth under the federal Youth Employment and Demonstration Projects Act.[66]

The below-average employment rates of poor adolescents who are beyond the age of required high school attendance are attributable to a combination of somewhat lower rates of labor force participation and sharply higher rates of unemployment. Estimated unemployment rates for the combined population of high school students was ap-

CHART 18A

Employment/Population Ratios of 16 to 19 Year Old High School Students, By Family Income and Race/Ethnicity, 1980

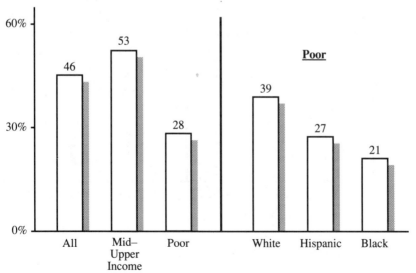

proximately 27 percent in 1980; however, poor adolescents experienced unemployment rates in the 30–50 percent range, two to three times as high as those faced by their counterparts with higher family income (Chart 18B). Poor black adolescents were at greatest risk of unemployment, with a majority of these labor force participants unsuccessful in finding jobs at the time of both surveys.

The labor market situation for teens deteriorated substantially in the early part of the 1980s, with sharp rises in unemployment and declines in labor force participation occurring between early 1979 and mid-1983 as the economy experienced its sharpest slowdown since the Depression of the 1930s.[67] While labor market conditions have improved since then, employment rates for sixteen-to-nineteen year old high school students had not fully recovered to their early 1979 values by 1988. At the time of the March 1988 CPS survey, approximately one-third of sixteen-to-nineteen year old students were reported to be employed (Chart 19A).[68] Only one-sixth of the students from poor families were reported to be working versus 40 percent of those in upper income families. Again, poor black adoles-

CHART 18B

**U.S. Unemployment Rates of 16 to 19 Year Old
Poor High School Students, 1980**

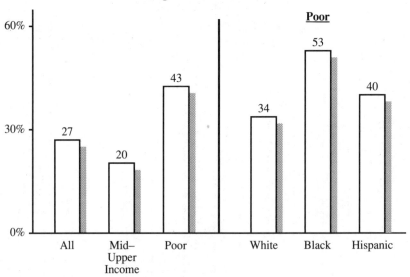

*Source: National Longitudinal Survey of Youth Market Experience, 1979 and 1980
interviews.*

CHART 19A

U.S. Employment-to-Population Ratios of 16 to 19 Year Old High School Students, 1988

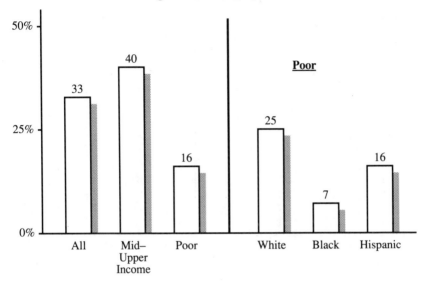

cents were least likely to be working (7%), followed by Hispanics (16%) and whites (25%). High unemployment rates among poor adolescents were more responsible than limited labor force participation for these results (Chart 19B).[69]

The impacts of more limited in-school employment experiences of poor adolescents are not simply confined to the high school years. High school students with more substantial work experience tend to be employed more often in the early years following graduation, and their in-school work experience has favorable effects on wages in the early post-high school period.[70] These findings hold true for whites and blacks.[71] Thus, poor youth will enter the labor market in their late teens with less work experience, less formal schooling, and more limited academic and vocational skills than their more affluent counterparts. These lower levels of human capital development place them at a severe disadvantage in the labor market.

While work experience during high school does favorably influence the early transition from school to work, especially for those students not enrolling in college, there have been concerns about the effects of in-school employment upon the school attendance and academic performance of students, especially for those working more than twenty hours per week while in school.[72] A recent analysis by the

CHART 19B

**U.S. Unemployment Rates of 16 to 19 Year Old
High School Students, 1988**

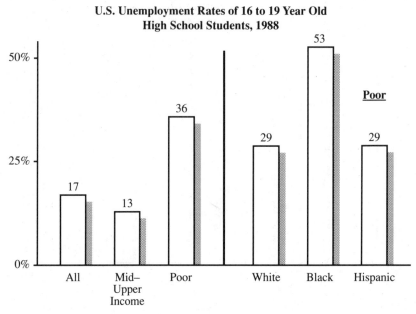

Source: March 1988 CPS Public Use Tape.

Educational Testing Service of the relationships between work, literacy, and academic performance of high school juniors indicates that in-school employment on average does *not* appear to have any adverse impacts upon the academic performance or school behavior of students.[73] While students who work more than twenty hours per week are characterized by below average academic skills, lower participation in college preparatory programs, and less time spent on homework, the adverse relationship to work hours tends to disappear when other relevant background variables and educational expectations are controlled for. Similar findings were reported in a longitudinal analysis of the relationships between in-school employment experiences and the academic performance of high school students over the 1979–1982 period.[74]

Given their greater tendency to leave high school without a diploma, their lower likelihood of attending college immediately after graduation, and their more difficult labor market entry, youth from poor families are more likely to be neither enrolled in school nor employed in their late teens.[75] In March 1988, slightly under 10 percent of all sixteen-to-nineteen year old civilians were neither enrolled in school nor employed (Chart 20). One-fourth of poor adolescents fell into this category while only 4 percent of those in families with high-incomes were neither engaged in a schooling activity nor employed. Although this category contains a dispropor- tionate number of poor female adolescents with parenting responsi- bilities, both poor young men and poor young women are considera- bly less likely than their more affluent counterparts to be employed or in school in these critical "investment years" which will significantly influence adult labor market participation and earnings potential.

The Early Transition from School to Work

The transition from high school to the world of work by non-college bound youth is neither a smooth nor an easy one for many; however, the early adjustment problems are much more severe for poor youth, dropouts, and a number of disadvantaged minorities. The literature on the school-to-work transition process, especially for men, notes that the transition from school to the adult, career-oriented labor market takes place in stages rather than in one step shortly after high

CHART 20

Percent of 16 to 19 Year Olds Who Were Neither Employed Nor Enrolled in School, By Family Income and Race/Ethnicity, 1988

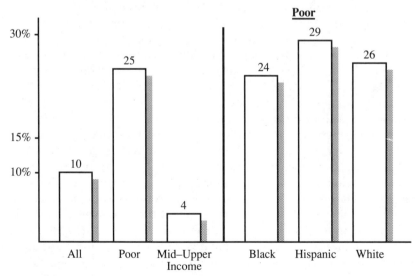

Source: March 1988 CPS public use tape.

school graduation. One analyst has referred to the first, or "early," stage of the transition process as a period of "floundering," which most youth must pass through before they settle on a path to the career employment that will provide an adequate earnings stream.[76] Others have called this first phase one of "search and trial work," which for most white males is completed around age twenty-five.[77] This early transition period also has been characterized as an employment "moratorium period" analogous to Erikson's classification of adolescence as a psychosocial moratorium stage.[78] This moratorium period is followed by a settling down period associated with career identification, job stability, and marriage.

The length of time needed by young adults to pass through these stages of exploration to career employment appears to be increasing over the years. Poor young adults have a particularly difficult time in establishing any type of substantive niche in the labor market during this early transition period. A review of the labor force and employment status of non-enrolled seventeen-to-twenty year olds as of March 1988 reveals the rather precarious labor market position of poor youth quite clearly (Chart 21).[79] Of all seventeen-to-twenty year old males who had completed twelve or fewer years of school and who were not attending any school program, approximately 86 percent were participating in the civilian labor force, 70 percent were employed, and 52 percent occupied full-time jobs.[80]

Poor youth made up a disproportionate share of those doing badly in this early transition process. While nearly three of every four poor males were either working or looking for work, only 46 percent of all those looking were successful in obtaining a job, and only three of ten held a full-time job. Full-time job-holding rates rose consistently with the family income backgrounds of these youth, reaching 64 percent for those young men living in a family with high-income.

Young women living in poor families (almost all of these teenaged women are still living at home with parents or other relatives) have an even more tenuous relationship with the labor market and face formidable problems in obtaining access to full-time jobs when they do seek work. Child-raising responsibilities of poor young women are partly responsible for their more limited attachment to the labor market. Only half of the non-enrolled seventeen-to-twenty year old women from poor families were active in the labor force in March 1988, and more than one-third of these women were unemployed. As a consequence of their more limited labor force attachment and their above-average rate of unemployment, barely one-third of this group were employed in March 1988, and only one-half of the employed held full-time jobs. The limited work experience of poor women

CHART 21

**Employment Experience of Non-Enrolled 17 to 20 Year Olds
With No Post-Secondary Education, 1988**

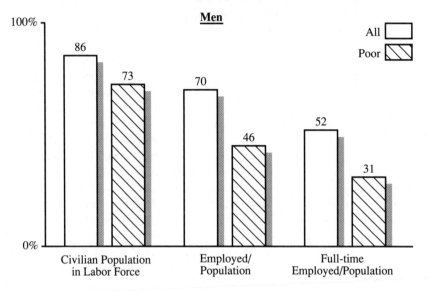

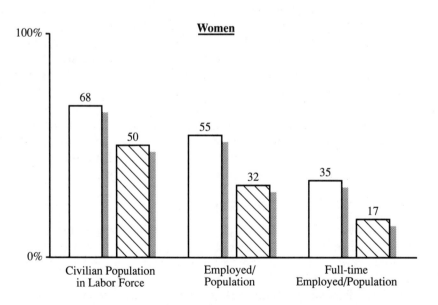

Source: March 1988 CPS Public Use Tape.

during the early adult years will significantly reduce their earnings potential in their late adult years and make the escape from poverty more difficult.[81]

The characteristics of the jobs obtained by poor young adults also tend to differ in a number of substantive ways from those held by their more affluent counterparts. During 1987, 60 percent of all non-enrolled seventeen-to-twenty year olds were employed by firms in the retail trade and service industries.[82] Retail trade firms alone accounted for 39 percent of the jobs held by these youth, and eating and drinking establishments, including many fast food restaurants, employed one of every six such youth. Employed young adults from poor families are even more concentrated in the retail trade and service industries. Two-thirds of them worked in such industries during 1987, with retail trade accounting for 43 percent of their jobs. Eating and drinking establishments alone employed one of every four poor young adults. Only one of six of these poor young adults held a job in construction or manufacturing industries, and the public administration sector was the source of employment for only one of every 100 poor young adults.

Research has shown that a disproportionate share of the jobs filled by young adults is in small establishments—that is, those with fewer than twenty-five employees.[83] Such jobs are less likely to provide non-wage benefits such as health insurance. Employed poor young adults also are highly concentrated in a few major occupational groups. In 1987, approximately five of every nine of them worked in service occupations, as laborers/handlers, or as cashiers. Food service workers made up nearly one-fifth of the employed poor. Young adults living in high-income families were far less dependent on these lower-skilled occupations. Only 35 percent of them held jobs as service workers, laborers or cashiers. Another 38 percent of these youth were employed as professional/technical/managerial workers, skilled blue collar workers, or in administrative support office) occupations. By contrast, only 19 percent of employed poor young adults were able to secure these more highly-skilled white and blue collar jobs.

Transition to the Career Labor Market

The more limited labor market exposure of poor young adults during their adolescent years and their more frequent lack of a high school diploma confines them to the "youth labor market" for a major part of their early adulthood.[84] Normally, as young people move from their teenage years into their twenties, they typically search for more stable, career jobs.[85] These jobs are characterized by an increased informal, if not formal, commitment between employer and employee. In return for satisfactory performance on the job, firms will provide more substantial amounts of on-the-job training and often will offer health insurance and other key employee benefits that are designed in part to secure the loyalty of workers and thus a stable work force. During these early years of entry into career labor markets, many young adults can also look forward to relatively steep increments in real annual earnings.[86]

Over the past fifteen years, the transition from the youth labor market to career labor markets has become a more prolonged and tortuous one for an increasing number of young adults, especially those with no post-secondary schooling. Young persons are finding it more difficult to secure stable, career jobs than was the case in the tighter labor markets of the mid- to late-1960s and much of the early 1970s. Higher proportions of the young adult population are spending a fairly long time in that segment of the labor market typically regarded as the "teen or youth labor market." One major consequence is that inflation-adjusted annual earnings have actually *declined* for some subgroups of our nation's young adult population, particularly those with no post-secondary schooling. In 1987, mean real annual earnings of non-enrolled twenty to twenty-four year olds were 12 percent below those of 1973. For young adults overall, the decline was concentrated among young males, where real annual earnings declined by nearly 25 percent.The real earnings of young females posted a $630 gain, or 9.2 percent increase, over this period (Chart 22). This increase was driven by increased labor force attachment, not higher hourly wages.

The factors underlying the divergent trends in male and female earnings are numerous. Among males, higher proportions with zero reported earnings, decreases in year-round full-time work, and lower real hourly earnings have all contributed to the real annual earnings decline.[87] The estimated increase in the mean real annual earnings of young women over the period is primarily attributable to increased labor force attachment and more hours of employment during the year. The median nominal weekly wages of young women employed full-time did not keep pace with the rate of inflation over the 1973–1987 period.[88]

For both young male and female adults, levels of real annual earnings have become even more strongly associated with formal educational attainment in recent years. The degree to which young men were able to avoid suffering from the effects of sharp changes in real earnings varied considerably by the amount of formal schooling completed. As a group, male high school dropouts showed the largest

CHART 22

Mean Real Earnings of Non-Enrolled 20 to 24 Year Olds
By Educational Attainment, 1973 and 1987
(In 1987 dollars)

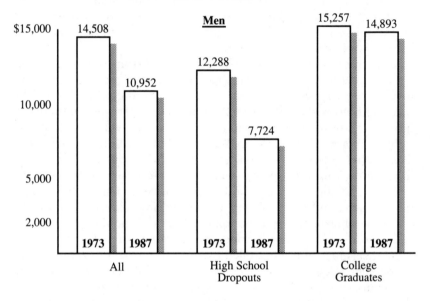

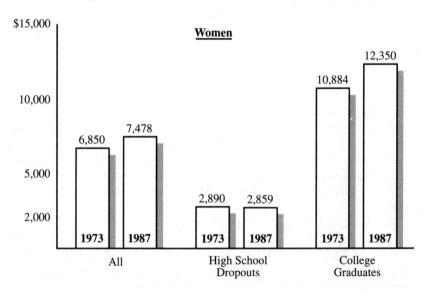

Source: March 1974 and March 1988 CPS Public Use Tape.

absolute and relative decline in real annual earnings (37%), followed by male high school graduates (28%), those males with some college (20%), and finally, male college graduates (2%). Among young females, school dropouts failed to show any real annual earnings improvements at all, while young female college graduates achieved mean real annual earnings in 1987 that were nearly 14 percent higher than those of 1973.

The extremely low annual earnings of female high school dropouts is attributable in part to their sharply lower rates of attachment to the labor force. During 1987, only 51 percent of those young women who lacked a high school diploma worked at some point during the year, versus 82 percent of high school graduates and 96 percent of college graduates. Even when they were employed, young female dropouts achieved mean annual earnings only 63 percent as high as that of high school graduates and 43 percent of that of college graduates. The economic returns to formal schooling and experience for young women appear to have improved considerably during the past decade, leaving those without such schooling and experience even further behind than before.[89]

YOUNG ADULTS AND POVERTY:
THE EXTENSION OF ECONOMIC ADOLESCENCE

The household living arrangements of the nation's poor young adults (excluding students and a small number who were serving in the armed forces) are depicted in Chart 23. Only slightly more than four of every ten of these poor young adults had formed their own families (or unrelated subfamilies) and were either the family head or spouse of the family head. Another 35 percent were still living at home with their parents or another relative, and the remaining 24 percent were living on their own or with friends. Poor young adult women were considerably more likely than men to have formed their own family (as head or spouse) while poor males were more likely to be living at home with their parents (43%) or on their own (35%). Both poor black (47%) and Hispanic (40%) young adults were considerably more likely than whites to be living with their parents or other relatives.

These young adults are poor for a variety of reasons. Single parents and spouses with children are often out of the labor force altogether or have very sporadic labor force attachment. Poor males are more likely to be participating in the labor force, but they experience severe difficulties in obtaining access to stable, year-round employment and career jobs that pay higher wages and provide substantive on-the-job

CHART 23

Household Living Arrangements of
Poor U.S. 20–24 Year Olds

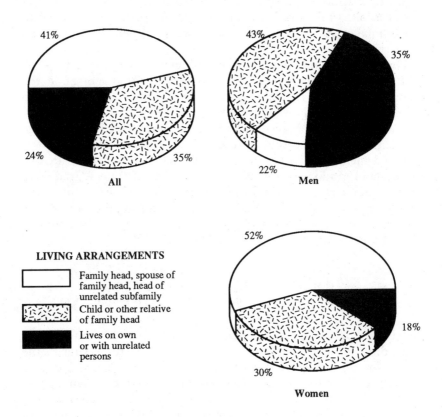

LIVING ARRANGEMENTS

Family head, spouse of
family head, head of
unrelated subfamily

Child or other relative
of family head

Lives on own
or with unrelated
persons

Source: March 1988 CPS Public Use Tapes.

training opportunities. Employed poor men and women are frequently confined to relatively low skilled, low-wage positions that often
resemble teen labor market jobs. In sum, these young adults have far
lower incomes than what is required to support them adequately in
separate living quarters.

Of the 15.1 million non-enrolled young adults (twenty to twenty-
four years old) in 1988, 2.6 million, or 17 percent, were members of
poor households. Five of every six of these poor young adults had
completed only twelve or fewer years of schooling at the time of the

March 1988 CPS survey.[90] While nearly eight of every ten poor young male adults were active participants in the civilian labor force, only 58 percent of them were successful in obtaining employment, representing an unemployment rate of 26.5 percent for labor force participants, nearly three times as high as that of non-poor twenty to twenty-four year olds. Full-time employment was even more scarce than employment generally. Only 39 percent of poor male adults held a full-time job.

Less than half (44%) of young poor female adults were participating in the civilian labor force during March 1988, and only three of ten were employed. Part-time jobs were more frequent among poor women; only one of six of such women were holding a full-time job. Their full-time employment/population ratio was only one-third to one-fourth as high as that of their more affluent counterparts.

Poor young adults with no post-secondary schooling are especially unlikely to be employed at any point in time, and the character of their employment experiences during the year tends to differ substantially from those of the non-poor. Among all non-enrolled young adult males with no post-secondary schooling, a slight majority (52%) were able to secure full-time employment for fifty to fifty-two weeks. Only one of seven young adult men living in poverty households were employed full-time, year-round during that year, a fact that obviously contributed to the low incomes of their households. Poor male school dropouts were the least likely (10%) to be in year-round, full-time employment.

Only one-third of young adult women with no post-secondary schooling were employed full-time, year-round during 1987, and the pattern of findings by household income is quite similar to that for young men. Of the young women in poverty households, only 5 percent worked year-round, full-time, during 1987. Increasing the labor market attachment of poor young adults, and their access to jobs providing more stable, year-round employment opportunities, are key to reducing poverty. Recent findings from the Survey of Income and Program Participation reveal that eighteen to twenty-four year-olds had the highest exit rate from poverty at mid-decade and that poor persons moving from part-year to year-round, full-time employment were the most successful in escaping from poverty.[91]

Characteristics of Jobs Held by Poor Young Adults

Not only are poor young adults considerably less likely than their higher income counterparts to be working full-time, year-round, but they also tend to occupy jobs in less well-compensated industrial sectors and occupational groups (Chart 24). Poor young adults (both male and female) are over-represented in farm/forestry, retail trade, and service industries—especially those outside of the relatively high-paying professional services. Approximately 56 percent of employed poor men and 80 percent of employed poor women were working in such industries during 1987.[92] The fraction of young men and women holding jobs in such industries tends to decline as household income rises. The concentration of the poor in such industries has important human capital implications. Few registered apprenticeships exist in such sectors, and formal company training programs are considerably more likely to be focused on those workers with college degrees.[93] Limited on-the-job and off-site training opportunities for poor young adults further reduces the relative stock of human capital that they will possess in their later adult years and, thus, the expected growth rate of their future earnings.

As would be expected, employed poor young adults also are over-represented in lower skilled occupations. During 1987, 35 percent of employed young males held jobs as farm/forestry workers, service workers, laborers, handlers, and cleaners. Nearly half of the employed young men from poor households were working in such occupations, a ratio nearly twice as high as the share of employed young men in households with incomes three or more times the poverty line. Similar patterns apply to the findings for employed young women. A slight majority (51%) of poor employed women held jobs as farm, service, or laborer/cleaner/handler workers while only one of five employed women in households with incomes three or more times the poverty line did so.

Weekly Earnings

It has been noted that changes in the job and wage structure of the national economy have led to an extension of the period of economic adolescence in American society over the past fifteen years, especially for non-college educated young adults.[94] Changes in both the real absolute and relative weekly wage position of young male adults employed full-time over the past twenty years illustrate this trend in a straightforward manner. During 1967, the median weekly wage of eighteen to twenty-four year old males working full-time was equivalent to nearly 74 percent of the median weekly wage of all full-time employed adult males (age twenty-five and over).[95] As the labor market absorbed increasing numbers of young adults from the baby boom generation over the following decade, the relative weekly wage

CHART 24

Non-Enrolled 20 to 24 Year Olds Employed in
Selected Industries and Occupations, 1987

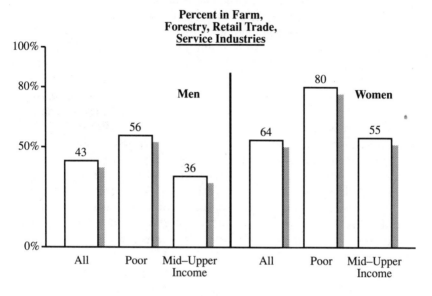

Percent in Farm,
Forestry, Retail Trade,
Service Industries

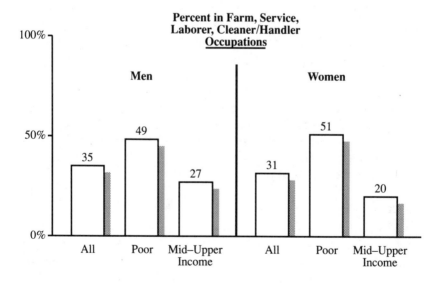

Percent in Farm, Service,
Laborer, Cleaner/Handler
Occupations

Source: March 1988 CPS Public Use Tape.

position of young males deteriorated, falling to 62 percent by the second quarter of 1979.[96] Over the next three years, a combination of two national economic recessions and a major downsizing of employment in a number of basic manufacturing industries drove the relative weekly wage position of full-time employed young adult males down to 54 percent of the median weekly wage for adult males.

Despite six years of continuous employment growth, falling unemployment for young adults, and a diminished supply of eighteen to twenty-four year olds, the real median weekly wage of full-time employed eighteen to twenty-four year old males has failed to increase.[97] The 1988 relative weekly wage position of these young men remained at 54 percent of the median of full-time adult males.[98] This substantial downward movement in the relative weekly wage position of young male adults, combined with the 29 percent decline in their real weekly wages since 1973, provide marked evidence of the lengthening of the transition from adolescence to economic adulthood in American society. Within this context, poor young adults largely are "adults" in name only, often far removed from the career jobs in mainstream labor markets whose occupancy represents a true rite of passage to economic adulthood.

Given the lower amounts of formal schooling and the more limited literacy proficiencies of poor young adults and their more frequent confinement to part-time and lower-skilled jobs, one would expect their weekly earnings to be considerably below those of their employed counterparts from more affluent households. Estimates of the March 1988 median weekly earnings of all employed twenty to twenty-four year old persons not simultaneously enrolled in school are presented in Chart 25.[99]

Median weekly earnings of young adults from poor households ($150) were at the bottom of the distribution, and median weekly earnings rose consistently with family income. Those young adults living in households with 1987 incomes three or more times the poverty line had median weekly earnings of $276, an earnings level 84 percent above that of poor young adults.

Health Insurance, Pension Coverage and Unionization

The economic rewards from work often go well beyond the wages and salaries provided by the employer. The availability of health insurance and pension benefits has become an important determinant of the current and future economic well-being of workers and their families. Poor young adults unfortunately are the least likely to be covered by any form of health insurance, including Medicaid, and

CHART 25

**Median Weekly Earnings of Employed 20 to 24 Year Olds
Not Enrolled in School, By Family Income, 1988**

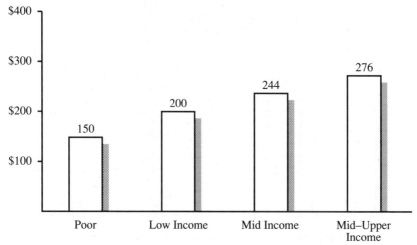

Source: March 1988 CPS Public Use Tape.

they seldom are eligible for coverage under an employer-sponsored pension plan when they do work (Chart 26).

The absence of health insurance coverage for thirty-five to forty million Americans is the major shortcoming of America's health care delivery system.[100] Young adults (twenty to twenty-four) are the least likely to be covered by any form of health insurance, including a health insurance plan of another household member or Medicaid.[101] Poor young male adults are the most likely to lack health insurance coverage, with only 43 percent of twenty to twenty-four year old males in poor households having some form of health insurance coverage during that year. The low rate of coverage for such men is a result of both their lower rates of employment and the absence of employer-financed group health insurance plans in the firms in which they are employed. Poor young women also experience lower rates of health insurance (65%) than their more affluent counterparts; however, they are more likely than poor young men to be covered by health insurance, primarily due to their greater receipt of Medicaid benefits in conjunction with their status as recipients of Aid to Families with Dependent Children.[102]

Employed young men and women are seldom covered by company-sponsored pension plans. During 1987, fewer than one in five employed twenty to twenty-four year olds was covered by a company-

CHART 26

Health Insurance Coverage, Pension Plan Coverage and Unionization Status of all 20 to 24 Year Olds, By Sex and Poverty Status, 1988

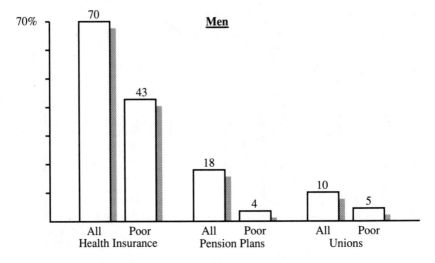

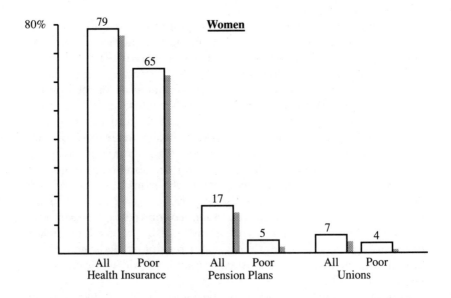

Source: March 1988 CPS Public Use Tape.

funded pension plan. This low rate of pension coverage was primarily due to the absence of such plans in the firms in which young adults worked; however, even when such plans did exist, young workers were less likely to be eligible for coverage due to limited job tenure and part-time employment. Employed poor young adults were the least likely to be covered by a pension plan, with only 4 to 5 percent of poor men and women reporting such coverage during 1987.

The shifting industrial distribution of the jobs obtained by young men and women combined with the continued low rates of unionization in many retail trade and private service industries also have reduced the proportion of young workers that are union members or covered by the provisions of a collective bargaining agreement. During March 1988, only 10 percent of employed young males and 7 percent of employed young female adults were either members of labor unions or holding jobs whose wages, fringes, and/or working conditions were influenced by the provisions of an existing collective bargaining agreement.[103] Both of these ratios were well below those for older workers, with young men being only one-third as likely as thirty-five to fifty-four year old males to be members of unions or covered by the terms of a collective bargaining agreement.

Employed young adults from poverty households were the least likely to be employed in a unionized job setting. Only 5 percent of employed poor males and 4 percent of employed poor women were working in an establishment that was unionized (Chart 26). The extremely limited presence of unions in the firms employing poor young adults also tends to reduce the real wages that they receive and the adequacy of their fringe benefit packages. Being a member of a labor union typically tends to raise the real earnings of young workers, especially those with no post-secondary schooling.[104]

The employment problems of America's young adult poverty population thus are not simply confined to their difficulties in securing a job at any point in time or to their sharply reduced chances of obtaining year-round, full-time employment. When employed, the young working poor also are considerably more likely to be found in firms on the periphery of the economy (small firms, retail trade, lower-level service firms) and in jobs that are relatively unskilled and less tied to formal training and internal career mobility paths.[105] The employment experiences of many of the young adult poor thus are weakly connected to mainstream career labor markets. The concentration of poor young workers in firms at the periphery of the economy (the secondary labor market) can also reduce the economic returns that they receive from formal schooling and experience.[106] Their low hourly and weekly earnings, the frequent absence of health insurance and pension benefits, and the extremely limited presence of unions in the work place are visible symbols of the marginal and "contingent" nature of the employment opportunities made available to the young adult poor.[107]

New Directions for Employment Policy

Sustained improvements in the real earnings position of poor young adults are critical to national goals of reducing future poverty and dependence and strengthening the capacity of young adults to marry and form stable families.[108] The success of such efforts will not only be dependent on intensifying investments in the basic academic and functional literacy proficiencies and vocational skills of the existing young adult poor, but also a restructuring of the system of economic rewards from work. Changes in the supply side characteristics of the poor young adult population are clearly needed to boost work performance and potential productivity.[109] At the same time, however, a reorganization of existing job responsibilities, internal job structures, company training investments, and the expected real compensation streams from work also will be needed to guarantee that such human capital investments in the poor do lead to sufficient economic payoffs to themselves and to society at large.[110]

The latter demand side changes and the restructuring of work responsibilities and training opportunities are likely to be essential to efforts to increase the economic and social rewards (wages, benefits, social status) from work for the poor.[111] With few exceptions,[112] (such as the previous New Careers programs), the employment-oriented anti-poverty policies of the federal government have emphasized changes in the human capital traits of the poor rather than changes in job content, the job structure, or the existing compensation system.[113] A better blend of policies seems to be clearly needed as we move into the last decade of the twentieth century.

NOTES

1. While there are seldom sharp changes in the characteristics and behavior of youth as one moves slightly above this poverty income threshold, the size of the differences between the characteristics, economic and social environments, and schooling/employment experiences of subgroups of adolescents tend to widen considerably as one moves up the socioeconomic ladder. To illustrate the magnitude and nature of these differences, we

frequently compare the situation of poor youth with that of adolescents and young adults in other income categories. For a review of the family income poverty guidelines of the federal government, *see* U.S. Department of Commerce, Bureau of the Census, Current Population Reports, Consumer Income Series P-60, No. 166, *Money Income and Poverty Status in the United States, 1988.* Washington, D.C., 1989.

2. Kathleen M. White and Joseph C. Speisman, *Adolescence* (Belmont, WA: Wadsworth Publishing Company, 1977). In Erikson's life cycle model, adolescence and the early adult transition typically appear to occupy the fourteen to twenty-one age period. Yet, as Erikson himself has noted, the length of this stage of psychosocial moratorium can vary from one individual to another. ". . . the delay of adulthood can be prolonged and intensified to a forceful and fateful degree." In Levinson's model, adolescence begins around age thirteen and continues to about seventeen-to-eighteen, at which point the stage of early adult transition begins. In this model the movement from adolescence to full adulthood is a much lengthier process than previous life cycle models have suggested. *See* Erik H. Erikson, "Youth: Fidelity and Diversity," in *The Challenge of Youth* (Garden City, NY: Doubleday and Company, Inc., 1965): 1–28. *See* Daniel J. Levinson, et. al., *The Seasons of a Man's Life* (New York, NY: Alfred A. Knopf, 1985).

3. The fourteen to twenty-one definition also has been adopted by the U.S. Congress in its enactment of national employment and training legislation, including the current Job Training Partnership Act and its predecessor the Comprehensive Employment and Training Act. In its 1974 report, The Panel on Youth of the President's Science Advisory Committee referred to youth as those fourteen to twenty-four years old. These years were seen as the interval during which children are transformed into adults. By age twenty-four, the transition to the adult labor market by most youth was believed to be complete. Finally, The W.T. Grant Foundation Commission on Work, Family and Citizenship focused on the economic and social status and the developmental needs of sixteen to twenty-four year old youth who do not go to college. In its interim report, the Commission described the "Forgotten Half" as "the approximately 20 million sixteen to twenty-four year olds who are not likely to embark upon undergraduate education." *See* National Commission on Youth, *The Transition of Youth to Adulthood: A Bridge Too Long* (Boulder, CO: Westview Press, 1980). *See*, Report of the Panel on Youth of the President's Science Advisory Committee, *Youth: Transition to Adulthood* (Chicago, IL: The University of Chicago Press, 1974). *See* William T. Grant Foundation Commission on Work, Family, and Citizenship, *The Forgotten Half: Non-College Youth in America* (Washington, D.C., 1988).

4. Gordon Berlin and Andrew M. Sum, *Toward a More Perfect Union: Basic Skills, Poor Families, and Our Economic Future,* Ford Foundation, New York, 1988; Clifford Johnson and Andrew M. Sum, *Declining Earnings of Young Men: Their Impact on Poverty, Adolescent Pregnancy, and Family Formation,* (Children's Defense Fund, Washington, D.C., 1987); Andrew M. Sum and Neal Fogg, *Labor Market Turbulence and the Employment and Earnings Experiences of Young*

Adult Males: Implications for National Workforce Preparedness, Report Prepared for the National Planning Association Work Group on Workforce Preparedness, 1989; Andrew M. Sum and Neal Fogg, *The Changing Economic Fortunes of Young Black Men in the New American Economy*, Paper Prepared for the U.S. Congress, House Committee on Children, Youth, and Families, Washington, D.C., 1989; Andrew M. Sum, Robert Taggart and Neal Fogg, *Withered Dreams: The Declining Economic Fortunes of American Non-College Educated Males and Their Families*, Report Prepared for The William T. Grant Foundation Commission on Work, Family and Citizenship, Washington, D.C., 1988.

5. U.S. Bureau of the Census, 1989.

6. Frank Levy, *Poverty and Economic Growth*, Report Prepared for the Ford Foundation Project on Social Welfare and the American Future, (New York, NY, 1986); Frank Levy, *Dollars and Dreams: The Changing American Income Distribution* (Russell Sage Foundation, New York, NY, 1987).

7. The adolescent population described in these charts excludes all individuals living in institutions (youth or adult correctional institutions, long-term hospitals) and all members of the armed forces living in barracks inside the U.S. or based overseas. The March 1980 CPS public use tape used sample weights based on population estimates prior to the availability of the 1980 Census results. The 1980 CPS estimates were later revised upward by the Census Bureau as new population benchmarks became available. The 1980 Census of Population revealed that there were approximately 23.8 million individuals thirteen-to-eighteen years old in the nation's civilian population.

8. The four race/ethnic groups appearing in Chart 1B and other charts throughout the text were defined in a manner that makes them mutually exclusive. Hispanic youth can be members of any race although the vast majority of them (97%) report themselves as whites. Hispanic youth have been excluded from the count of whites, blacks, and "other" races. The "Other" group includes Asians, American Indians, and Alaskan natives.

9. Irwin Garfinkel and Sara S. McLanahan, *Single Mothers and Their Children: A New American Dilemma* (Washington, D.C.: The Urban Institute Press, 1986); Sar A. Levitan, Richard S. Belous and Frank Gallo, *What's Happening to the American Family?* (Revised Edition), (Baltimore, MD: The Johns Hopkins University Press, 1988); Harrell R. Rodgers, *Poor Women, Poor Families: The Economic Plight of America's Female-Headed Households* (Armonk, NY: M.E. Sharpe, Inc., 1986).

10. The fact that an adolescent lives in a married couple family does not automatically imply that he or she resides with both parents (or step-parents). Some of these adolescents can be living in a married couple family headed by a relative other than their parents, or they can be a member of a sub-family that is residing within a larger married couple family. For example, an adolescent could be living with his or her mother as a sub-family in a housing unit together with grandparents. Given the coding procedures used by the authors in classifying the family living arrangements of each adolescent, the above adolescent would be classified as living in a married couple family. In the overwhelming majority of cases, however, adolescents living in a married couple family are residing in a primary family with their parents.

11. The poverty status of adolescents living in subfamilies was based on subfamily income. Taking account of total money income of the entire family in which the subfamily resided makes the poverty rate about one percentage point lower in March 1988.

12. Other national research on the persistence of poverty has found that children living in families with absent fathers, blacks, and those with parents lacking a high school diploma are more likely to be members of the persistent poor population. The age groups of the children included in the analyses of long-term or persistent poverty tended to vary somewhat by study. Ellwood's analysis focused on the family poverty situation of children during the first ten years of their lives, while Adams and Duncan examined poverty conditions among children under eighteen in large urban areas of the nation. *See* Terry K. Adams and Greg J. Duncan, *The Persistence of Urban Poverty and Its Demographic and Behavioral Correlates*, Survey Research Center, Ann Arbor, MI: University of Michigan, 1988; Gordon Berlin, "The New Permanence of Poverty," in *The Ford Foundation Letter*, (New York, NY, vol. 19, no. 2, June 1988); David T. Ellwood, *Divide and Conquer: Responsible Security for America's Poor*, Ford Foundation Project on Social Welfare and the American Future, New York, NY, 1987.

13. The only age group with a lower exit rate out of poverty was the elderly; i.e., persons sixty-five years of age and older. Eighty-four percent of the elderly poor of 1984 were also poor in 1985. *See* U.S. Department of Commerce, Bureau of the Census, Current Population Reports, Household Economic Studies, Series P-60, no. 15, *Transitions in Income and Poverty Status: 1984–85* (Washington, D.C., 1989, p. 10).

14. The estimates of shifts in the incidence of poverty among adolescents in metropolitan and non-metropolitan areas over time are based on data for the vast bulk of the teenage population but not a complete 100 percent count. In 1974, the Census Bureau assigned a metropolitan status code to all respondents; however, in 1980, 8 percent of adolescents were not classified, and 15 percent were not classified in 1988 due to confidentiality restrictions.

15. According to recent Census Bureau population projections, the number of thirteen to eighteen year-olds, including members of the armed forces, is projected to increase from 20.1 million in mid-1990 to 21.9 million by 1995, and will rise further to 22.9 million by the year 2000. *See* Gregory Spencer, *Projections of the Population of the United States, by Age, Sex, and Race: 1988 to 2,080*, Report on Population Trends, U.S. Census Bureau, (Washington, D.C.: U.S. Government Printing Office, 1989).

16. The Center for Population Options has estimated that the taxpayer costs over a 20 year period associated with a birth to a teenage mother in 1987 would be $38,700. Center for Population Options, *Estimate of Public Cost for Teenage Childbearing in 1987*, Washington, D.C., 1988.

17. Between 1968 and 1988, the fraction of children in young primary families and subfamilies (head under 25 years of age) living with both parents present in the home has declined from 80 percent to 49 percent. Half of all children living in a family headed by a person under 25 years of age were

living in poverty in 1988. *See* Center for Labor Market Studies, *Social and Economic Indicators for Families With Children*, vol. 2, Prepared for Russell Sage Foundation, New York, NY, 1990.

18. Gordon Berlin and Andrew M. Sum, *Toward a More Perfect Union: Basic Skills, Poor Families, and Our Economic Future* (Ford Foundation, New York, NY, 1988); Karen Pittman, *Adolescent Pregnancy and Expanding Life Options: The Role of the Schools*, (Children's Defense Fund, Washington, D.C., 1986); *Preventing Adolescent Pregnancy: What Schools Can Do* (Children's Defense Fund, Washington, D.C. September 1986); and "Reading and Writing as Risk Reduction: The School's Role in Preventing Teenage Pregnancies," in *Teenage Pregnancy*, Diane J. Jones and Stanley F. Battle, eds., (New Brunswick, NJ: Transaction Publishers, 1990, pp. 55–70).

19. Frank F. Furstenburg, J. Brooks-Gunn, and S. Philip Morgan, *Adolescent Mothers in Later Life* (Cambridge, England: Cambridge University Press, 1987).

20. Furstenburg, et.al, *Adolescent Mothers*.

21. Andrew M. Sum and Frank Tortora, *Transitions in Poverty Status of America's Adolescents* (Center for Labor Market Studies, Northwestern University, Boston, 1990).

22. Berlin and Sum, *Toward a More Perfect Union*; Levy, *Dollars and Dreams*; Sum, Taggart, Fogg, *Withered Dreams*; W.T. Grant Foundation Commission on Work, Family, and Citizenship, *The Forgotten Half: Pathways to Success for America's Youth and Young Families* (Washington, D.C., 1988); Lawrence Mishel and David M. Frankel, *The State of Working America* (Economic Policy Institute, 1990–91 edition, Washington, D.C.).

23. Levy, *Dollars and Dreams*.

24. The groups actually being analyzed in this table consist of those respondents who were fourteen-to-fifteen years old and sixteen-to-seventeen years old at the time of the initial 1979 NLS survey and who were members of families with a 1978 money income below the federal government's poverty line for families of their size. The ASVAB test was administered during the summer of the following year (1980); thus, we simply added an additional year to their 1979 age. A number of these respondents may have had a birthday between the 1980 interview and the summer 1980 testing.

25. The AFQT test consists of four sub-parts of the Armed Services Vocational Aptitude Battery (ASVAB). The four sub-parts comprise approximately 63 minutes of the three-hour test. AFQT test scores can range from zero to a maximum of 105. *See* Berlin and Sum, *Towards a More Perfect Union*; Office of the Assistant Secretary of Defense, *Profile of American Youth: 1980 Nationwide Administration of the Armed Services Vocational Aptitude Battery*, Washington, D.C., March 1982; Andrew M. Sum, Paul E. Harrington, and William Goedicke, *Basic Skills of America's Teens and Young Adults: Findings of the 1980 National ASVAB Testing and Their Implications for Education, Employment, and Training Policies*, Report Prepared for the Ford Foundation, New York, NY, 1986.

26. AFQT test scores rise with age and additional years of schooling; thus, a separate distribution was estimated for seventeen-to-eighteen year olds.

The median test score of poor youth in this age range was 51, which falls at the 19th percentile of the distribution. While poor adolescents' basic academic proficiencies are located throughout the entire test score distribution, they are clearly over-represented in the bottom quintile of that distribution. A slight majority of poor fifteen-to-sixteen and seventeen-to-eighteen year olds fell into the bottom quintile of the AFQT test score distribution, and only 3 to 5 percent of them were represented in the top quintile. *See* William R. Morgan, "Schooling Effects of Youth from Public, Catholic, and Other Private High Schools," in *Pathways to the Future, Volume III*, Michael E. Borus, ed., (Center for Human Resource Research, Columbus OH: Ohio State University, 1983); Sum, Harrington, Goedicke, *Basic Skills of America's Teens and Young Adults*.

27. National Center for Education Statistics, *High School and Beyond, A National Longitudinal Study for the 1980's, Two Years In High School: The Status of 1980 Sophomores in 1982* (Washington, D.C.: U.S. Government Printing Office, 1984).

28. Samuel S. Peng, William B. Fetters, and Andrew J. Kolstad, *High School and Beyond: A National Longitudinal Study for the 1980's: A Capsule Description of High School Seniors* (U.S. Department of Education, Washington, D.C., 1981).

29. At the time of the 1979 NLS interview, between 6 and 7 percent of all fourteen-to-seventeen year old students were two or more years behind the modal grade for their age group. Rumberger's study indicates that about 4 percent of fourteen-to-seventeen year old students were two or more years behind modal grade at the time of the 1979 NLS interview. His analysis, however, is confined to those enrolled in grades 9–12 while ours includes junior high students, nearly all of whom are two or more years behind modal grade. Hispanics (15%) were most likely to fall into this category followed by blacks (12%) and whites (5%). Poor adolescents were considerably more likely than their more affluent counterparts to be two or more grades behind. Among all fourteen to twenty-two year olds enrolled in grades 9–12 in 1979, those students living in poor families were 3.4 times more likely than the non-poor to be two or more years behind modal grade. While 18 percent of the poor were two or more years behind modal grade, only 3 percent of the fourteen-to-seventeen year old adolescents living in families with incomes three or more times the poverty line were in this category. *See* Russell W. Rumberger, "Experiences in High School and College," *Pathways to the Future, Volume I*, Michael E. Borus, ed., Center for Human Resource Research, Columbus, OH: University of Ohio, 1980, p. 315. *See* Sum and Tortora, "AFQT Test Scores of 14–18 Year Olds."

30. Alfred G. Hess and James L. Greer, "Educational Triage and Dropout Rates," Paper Presented at the Annual Meeting of the American Educational Research Association, April 1986; Donald A. Rock et. al., *Study of Excellence in High School Education: Longitudinal Study, 1980–82, Final Report* (Educational Testing Service, Princeton, NJ, June 1985).

31. Michael E. Borus and Susan A. Carpenter, "Choices in Education," *Youth and the Labor Market* (W.E. Upjohn Institute for Employment Research,

Kalamazoo, MI, 1984, pp. 81–110); Michael E. Borus and Susan A. Carpenter, "Factors Associated with College Attendance of High School Seniors," *Economics of Education Review* 3 (1984): 169–176; Morgan, "Schooling Effects of Youth," 1983; William R. Morgan, "Quantity of Learning and Quality of Life for Public and Private High School Youth," in *Youth and the Labor Market* (W. E. Upjohn Institute for Employment Research, Kalamazoo, MI, 1984).

32. Borus and Carpenter, "Choices in Education," and "Factors Associated With College Attendance,"; Rumberger, "Experiences in High School and College,"; U.S. General Accounting Office, *School Dropouts: The Extent and Nature of the Problem* (Washington, D.C., June 1986).

33. Ronald D'Amico, "Informal Peer Networks as an Integrative and Social Control Mechanism," *Pathways to the Future, Volume III*, pp. 60–85; Morgan, "Schooling Effects of Youth"; Morgan, "Quantity of Learning."

34. The educational expectations data represent responses to the question, "How far in school do you think you will get?" Peng, et. al., *High School and Beyond*.

35. These percentages are based on the sample results weighted to reflect the national population of high school seniors, including those attending private schools.

36. Only 17 percent of those high school seniors with achievement test scores in the bottom quartile of the test score distribution expected to complete four years of college while 40 percent of those in the middle quartile and 82 percent of those in the top quartile expected to do so. Peng, et. al., *High School and Beyond*.

37. Berlin and Sum, *Towards a More Perfect Union, Pathways to the Future, Volume I;* Michael E. Borus, "A Description of Employed and Unemployed Youth in 1981," *Youth and the Labor Market* (The W.E. Upjohn Institute for Employment Research, Kalamazoo, MI, 1984, pp. 13–55); James Coleman, "Social Capital in the Creation of Human Capital," *American Journal of Sociology* 94 (1988): S95–S120; Andrew Hahn and Jacqueline Danzberger, *Dropouts In America: Enough Is Known For Action* (The Institute for Educational Leadership, Washington, D.C., 1987); Margaret Terry Orr, *Keeping Students in School* (San Francisco, CA: Jossey-Bass Publishers, 1987), and *What to Do About Youth Dropouts?* (Structural Employment/Economic Development Corporation, New York, NY, July 1987); Rumberger, "Experiences in High School and College"; U.S. General Accounting Office, *School Dropouts*.

38. A separate tracking of the school dropout behavior of sixteen-to-seventeen year old adolescents (in 1979) revealed quite similar patterns. Of those who were enrolled in school and had completed ten or fewer years of schooling at the time of the original 1979 NLS interview, 10 percent would leave school in the following year without a diploma. This group contains an above average share of students who were behind modal grade for their age group. The dropout rate is higher than would be expected for a completely representative sample of sixteen-to-seventeen year olds. Among poor adolescents in this age/schooling group, 23 percent withdrew from school versus only 7 percent of those with family incomes at least twice the poverty line.

Poor adolescents with above average basic academic skills were less than half as likely to withdraw from school as their poor counterparts with below average academic skills. *See* Andrew M. Sum, Neal W. Fogg and Sheila Palma, "Basic Academic Skills of Teenagers and Young Adults: Their Associations with Schooling Performance, School Dropout Behavior, Educational Attainment, and Labor Market Success," Statistical Package Prepared for the Commonwealth Futures Seminar, Brandeis University, December 1989.

Borus and Carpenter's analysis of the school dropout behavior of those fourteen to twenty-two year olds who were enrolled in school at the initial 1979 NLS interview provided similar findings. Slightly more than 5 percent of this group left school during the following year without completing the twelfth grade. Students living in poor families were 2.4 times as likely as the non-poor to drop out of school during this period. The findings of their multi-variate statistical analysis revealed that being a member of a poor family by itself did significantly increase the likelihood of dropping out. However, other key traits associated with living in a poverty environment, such as being two or more years behind modal grade, having low academic skills, not being enrolled in a college prep program, not expecting to complete college, being unemployed, and having parents with limited education, were also significant influences on school leaving. *See* Michael E. Borus and Susan A. Carpenter, "Choices in Education," *Youth and the Labor Market* (W.E. Upjohn Institute for Employment Research, Kalamazoo, MI, 1984, pp. 81–110).

The longitudinal tracking of 1980 sophomores included in the High School and Beyond Study has revealed that students from low SES family backgrounds and those with the weakest achievement test scores were most likely to drop out of school by the spring of 1982. Seventeen percent of the sophomores from the lowest quartile of the SES distribution had left school versus 9 percent of those in the middle two quartiles and only 5 percent in the top quartile. By the spring of 1984, nearly 38 percent of these dropouts would have obtained either a diploma or a GED; however, among both blacks and whites, those dropouts from low SES backgrounds were the least likely to have done so. *See* National Center for Educational Statistics, *High School and Beyond*; *See* Rock, et. al., *Study of Excellence in High School Education*. *See* Andrew Kolstad and Jeffrey A. Owings, "High School Dropouts Who Change Their Minds About School," (U.S. Department of Education, Washington, D.C., April 1986).

39. Some of those reporting twelve years of school may have a GED certificate rather than a high school diploma. Our analysis of 1979 and 1980 NLS data on this issue revealed that 98–99 percent of the respondents with twelve or more years of schooling indicated that they had a high school diploma.

40. Berlin and Sum, *Towards a More Perfect Union*, 1988; Robert Taggart, Andrew M. Sum, and Gordon Berlin, "Basic Skills: The Sine Qua Non," *Youth and Society* 19 (September 1987): 3–21; Sum, Harrington, and Goedicke, "Basic Skills of America Teens."

41. Morgan, Rock, et. al., *Study of Excellence*.

42. Kolstad and Owings, "High School Dropouts"; U.S. General Accounting Office, *School Dropouts*; Richard Venezky, Carl Kaestle, and Andrew M. Sum, *The Subtle Danger: Reflections on the Literacy Abilities of Young Adults*, Educational Testing Service, Princeton, NJ, 1987.

43. Sum, Harrington, and Goedicke, "Basic Skills"; Venezky, Kaestle, and Sum, *The Subtle Danger*.

44. Irwin S. Kirsch and Ann Jungeblut, *Literacy: Profiles of America's Young Adults*, Educational Testing Service, Princeton, NJ, 1986; William R. Morgan, "Quantity of Learning and Quality of Life for Public and Private High School Youth," *Youth and the Labor Market*, (W.E. Upjohn Institute for Employment Research, Kalamazoo, MI, 1984, pp. 111–156); Taggart, Sum, Berlin, "Basic Skills," pp. 3–21.

45. Paul E. Harrington and Andrew M. Sum, "Whatever Happened to the College Enrollment Crisis?," *Academe* 74 (September–October 1988): 17–22.

46. U.S. Department of Labor, Bureau of Labor Statistics, "Nearly Three-Fifths of the High School Graduates of 1988 Enrolled in College," Washington, D.C., June 29, 1989.

47. Charles F. Manski and David A. Wise, *College Choice in America* (Cambridge, MA: Harvard University Press, 1983); U.S. Department of Education, Office of Planning, Budget, and Evaluation, *College Enrollment Patterns of Black and White Students* (Washington, D.C., 1987).

48. The family poverty status of these 1979 high school seniors was based on their money income during calendar year 1978. Family income data were missing for approximately one-fifth of the students, but these students were included in the grand totals.

49. The Borus/Carpenter analysis is based on all respondents attending the twelfth grade in the spring of 1979 regardless of age or actual graduation status in the following year. Their estimated college attendance rate for this sample was 48 percent, nearly identical to our estimate (47%) for the slightly more restrictive sample. *See* Borus and Carpenter, "Factors Associated with College Attendance of High School Seniors," *Economics of Education Review* 3 (1984): 169–176.

50. The analysis used only a poverty/non-poverty status variable rather than several income breaks. The measure of academic ability was the respondent's score on a short world-of-work test rather than on the ASVAB or AFQT test scores.

51. The SES measure in this study is a composite index of five equally-weighted variables: father's education, mother's education, family income, father's occupation and household items. The elements of the index are based on the family situation of the respondent at the time of the 1980 interview.

52. Since some graduates will have transferred from one school to another over this period, the program sub-totals in charts 16A and 16B will exceed the total enrollment figures.

53. Due to the wording of the questions on the 1982 follow-up survey, one cannot precisely identify whether a student who withdrew had left before or

after completing a program. Given the limited time between graduation and the first follow-up, it is likely that the overwhelming majority left before completion.

54. Thirty-nine percent of 1980 high school seniors were enrolled in academic, graduate, or vocational courses at the time of the interview and 34 percent were taking academic or graduate courses. Only one of five seniors from low SES family backgrounds was enrolled in academic or vocational courses in the spring of 1984, and only one of six was in academic or graduate programs. In contrast, one of four seniors from the lower-middle SES quartile, three of eight from the upper-middle quartile, and five of eight from the top SES quartile were enrolled. These findings actually underestimated the overall size of the educational differentials among SES subgroups since 25 percent of the high SES seniors had obtained a two or four-year degree by the spring of 1984 versus only 5 percent of those from low SES backgrounds. The fields of study of those enrolled in academic courses also varied widely by SES subgroup, with the high SES students twice as likely as those from low SES backgrounds to be majoring in engineering, biology, and other physical science programs, the primary sources of the nation's future scientists and engineers. Taking into consideration the substantial difference between the proportions of students from high and low SES backgrounds enrolled in any type of academic program, we estimate that 12 percent of all high SES seniors were majoring in an engineering or physical science field versus only 2 percent of those from low SES family backgrounds. Calvin C. Jones, Susan Campbell, and Penny A. Sebring, *Four Years After High School: A Capsule Description of 1980 Seniors* (Washington, D.C.: U.S. Government Printing Office, 1986, p. 20).

Percent of 1980 High School Seniors Enrolled in Post-Secondary Education and Training Programs in Spring 1984, by Socioeconomic Status

	(A)	(B)
SES Group	Percent Taking Academic, Graduate or Vocational Courses	Percent Taking Academic or Graduate Courses
All	39	34
Lowest SES	21	16
Second Quartile SES	26	25
Third Quartile SES	42	37
Top Quartile SES	67	63

Source: Jones, et. al., *Four Years After High School: A Capsule Description of 1980 Seniors.*

Findings on the longer-term success rates of high school graduates in obtaining a bachelor's degree are available from a recent twelve-year analysis of the college transcripts of high school graduates from the Class of 1972. During the first twelve years following graduation from high school, 55 percent of the graduates attended a post-secondary school for one or more

years. Only 40 percent of the attendees obtained a bachelor's degree within
this period. Overall, two of nine graduates (22%) held a bachelor's degree by
the end of this period. *See* Paula R. Knepper, *Student Progress in College: NLS-
72 Post-Secondary Education Transcript Study, 1984*, U.S. Department of Education, Office of Educational Research and Improvement, Washington, D.C.,
February 1989.

**College Attendance Rates and Bachelor's Degree Attainment Rates for College
Attenders and All High School Graduates from the Class of 1972, by Family
Socioeconomic Status in High School**

	(A)	(B)	(C)
Socio-economic Status	Ever Attended College	Percent of Attendees Obtaining a Bachelor's Degree	Percent of High School Graduates With a Bachelor's Degree (A * B)
All	55.0	40.6	22.3
Low SES	35.5	25.7	9.1
Middle SES	52.3	34.8	18.2
High SES	80.5	54.8	44.1

Graduates from low SES family backgrounds were by far the least successful
in obtaining a bachelor's degree. Only 35 percent of low SES high school
graduates ever attended college, and, of those attending, a majority (52%)
did not complete more than one year of college. Only one-fourth of the post-
secondary students from low SES family backgrounds were successful in
obtaining a bachelor's degree by 1984. This rate was less than half that of
post-secondary students from high SES backgrounds. As a consequence of
their below-average college attendance and bachelor's degree attainment
rates, only 9 percent of high school graduates from low SES family backgrounds held a bachelor's degree twelve years after graduation. This ratio
compares quite unfavorably to the 18 percent of middle SES graduates and
the 44 percent of high SES graduates obtaining a bachelor's degree.

55. Robert E. Litan, Robert Z. Lawrence, and Charles L. Schultz, "Improving American Living Standards," *Critical Choices* (The Brookings Institution,
Washington, D.C., 1989, pp. 29–48); Sum, Taggart, Fogg, *Withered Dreams*.

56. Barbara Vobejda, "Class, Color and College," *The Washington Post,
National Weekly Edition*, 6 (May 15–21, 1989): 6–8.

57. The socio-economic status variable (SES) used in this analysis is an
index based on five variables reflecting the educational attainment, employment status, and occupational backgrounds of the parents of the student at
the time of the initial senior year interview. The achievement test scores are
based on a uniform reading and math test administered to respondents
during the senior year of high school.

58. Robert T. Michael and Nancy Brandon Tuma, "Youth Employment:

Does Life Begin At 16?," *The Journal of Labor Economics* 2 (October 1984): 464–476; Richard Santos, "The Employment Status of Youth," *Pathways to the Future, Volume I*, pp. 49–106.

59. Borus, "A Description of Employed Youth," pp. 13–55; Peng, et. al., *High School and Beyond*; Sum, Harrington, and Goedicke, "One-Fifth of the Nation's Teenagers," pp. 195–237.

60. The initial 1979 round of interviews took place between late January and August, although the vast majority were completed by May. While the NLS interviews were conducted with a sample of fourteen and fifteen year olds, the fifteen year olds were over-represented in the sample, accounting for nearly 59 percent of the combined sample of fourteen and fifteen year old respondents. *See* Borus, "A Description of Employed Youth," pp. 13–55.

61. Michael and Tuma, "Youth Employment," pp. 464–476; Santos, "The Employment Status of Youth," pp. 49–106.

62. Santos estimated that over half of the employed white females held jobs as baby-sitters and nearly one of every four white males held jobs as newspaper boys. *See* Santos, "The Employment Status of Youth," pp. 49–106.

63. Michael and Tuma, "Youth Employment," pp. 464–476.

64. The lower employment estimates of the CPS are primarily believed to be due to the use of proxy respondents (mothers responding for daughters/ sons rather than direct interviews with youth themselves) and to differences in survey administration. The estimated size of the discrepancies between the employment/population ratios of the CPS and direct surveys, such as the NLS, tend to fall as adolescents age, and they are typically smaller for out-of-school youth than for in-school youth. The March 1979 CPS estimates of employment rates for fourteen-to-fifteen year olds are typically 10 percentage points lower than those of the NLS. *See* Richard B. Freeman and James L. Medoff, "Why Does the Rate of Youth Labor Force Activity Differ Across Surveys?," in *The Youth Labor Market Problem: Its Nature, Causes, and Consequences*, Richard B. Freeman and David A. Wise, eds., (Chicago, IL: University of Chicago Press, 1982); Santos, "The Employment Status of Youth" pp. 49–106, and Santos, "Measuring the Employment Status of Youth—A Comparison of the Current Population Survey and the National Longitudinal Survey," *Proceedings of the Thirty-Third Annual Meetings*, (Industrial Relations Association, Madison, WI, 1982, pp. 62–68).

65. Only those sixteen-to-nineteen year olds who had completed fewer than twelve years of school and who were enrolled in school at the time of the interview were included in our analysis.

66. Andrew Hahn and Robert Lerman, *What Works in Youth Employment Policy?*, (Committee on New American Realities, Washington, D.C., 1985); Andrew Sum and Paul Simpson, "The Deteriorating Employment Position of American Teenagers: Implications for National Employment & Training Policy," (Report Prepared for the Center for Income & Employment Studies, Boston, MA: Brandeis University, 1982).

67. Sum, Harrington, Goedicke, "One-Fifth of the Nation's Teenagers," pp. 195–237.

68. Again, the CPS estimates of employment rates for sixteen-to-nineteen year olds have been found to be 6–7 percentage points below those of the NLS. *See* Santos, "The Employment Status of Youth," 1980, pp. 49–106, and Santos, "Measuring the Employment Status of Youth," 1982, pp. 62–68.

69. The more limited job prospects for poor adolescents are not confined to any one month. Analysis of the 1987 work experience data for these sixteen-to-nineteen year old students revealed that those adolescents living in poor families were employed on average for 60 percent fewer weeks and earned 70 percent less than their counterparts in families with incomes three or more times the poverty line.

70. Irwin Herrnstadt, Morris A. Horowitz, and Andrew M. Sum, *The Transition from School to Work: The Contribution of Cooperative Education Programs at the Secondary Level*, (Report Prepared for U.S. Department of Labor, Employment and Training Administration, Office of Research and Development, Washington, D.C., 1979); Meyer and Wise, *The Transition from School to Work* and "High School Preparation," pp. 277–348; Stanley P. Stephenson, "The Transition from School to Work with Job Search Implications," *Conference Report on Youth Unemployment: Its Measurement and Meaning*, (Washington, D.C.: U.S. Government Printing Office, 1980, pp. 65–85); Wayne Stevenson, "The Relationship Between Early Work Experience and Future Employability," in *The Lingering Crisis of Youth Unemployment*, Arvil Adams and Garth Mangum, eds., (W.E. Upjohn Institute for Employment Research, Kalamazoo, MI, 1978).

71. Meyer and Wise, "High School Preparation," and *The Transition From School to Work*.

72. Ivan Charner and Bryna Shore Fraser, *Youth and Work* (The William T. Grant Foundation Commission on Work, Family, and Citizenship, Washington, D.C., 1987); Orr, *Keeping Students in School*, and *What to Do About Youth Dropouts?*

73. Barton's analysis is based on the findings of the 1986 National Assessment of Educational Progress (NAEP) survey of eleventh grade students. Approximately 29,000 high school juniors across the nation participated in the 1986 NAEP assessment. For a more comprehensive review of previous research findings on the relationships between in-school employment and school performance, *see* Charner and Fraser, *Youth and Work*; *see also*, Paul E. Barton, *Earning and Learning: The Academic Achievement of High School Juniors With Jobs*, (Educational Testing Service, Princeton, NJ, March 1989).

74. In a multi-variate statistical analysis of time use data from the 1981 NLS survey, D'Amico found that employed students did not have significantly different educational aspirations than those not working and that hours of work were significantly associated with lower educational aspirations only for white women. *See* Ronald D'Amico, "Informal Peer Networks as an Integrative and Social Control Mechanism," *Pathways to the Future, Volume III*, pp. 60–85.

75. The findings in this table apply only to the civilian non-institutional population of sixteen-to-nineteen year olds. Those young persons who were serving in the armed forces or members of the institutionalized population

(long-term hospitals, jails, prisons) were excluded from the totals. The CPS does not survey institutions, and only those members of the armed forces living off base in the U.S. can be identified on the March tape.

76. Stephen F. Hamilton, "Work and Maturity: Occupational Socialization of Non-College Youth in the United States and West Germany," *Research in the Sociology of Education and Socialization* 7 (1987): 287–312.

77. Marcia Freedman, "The Youth Labor Market," *From School to Work: Improving the Transition*, U.S. Government Printing Office, Washington, D.C., 1976, pp. 21–36.

78. Paul Osterman, *Getting Started: The Youth Labor Market* (Cambridge, MA: The MIT Press, 1980).

79. The population group in Chart 21 includes only members of the civilian non-institutional population, seventeen to twenty years of age. All members of the armed forces and inmates of institutions are excluded from the total. *See* Andrew Hahn and Robert Lerman, *What Works in Youth Employment Policy?*, (Committee on New American Realities, Washington, D.C., 1985).

80. The full-time employed are those working thirty-five or more hours per week during the reference week of the survey. Two or more jobs may have been held by such individuals.

81. The substantially lower employment rates of these poor seventeen-to-twenty year old adults were not confined to any one-month period. Analysis of the work experience data for the prior calendar year revealed that only 58 percent of these poor young men and women held a job for one or more weeks during 1987 versus 84 percent of the non-poor and nearly 94 percent of those living in families with incomes three or more times the poverty level. Fewer than one of every ten poor young adults worked year-round (fifty to fifty-two weeks) during 1987 while 42 percent of the non-poor did so. For a review of the influence of early work relationships, *see* Kristin A. Moore and Martha R. Burt, *Private Crisis: Public Cost: Policy Perspectives on Teenage Childbearing*, (Washington, D.C.: The Urban Institute Press, 1982).

82. The work experience supplement collects information on the industry and occupation of the longest job held by each respondent during the previous calendar year.

83. An analysis of unpublished May 1983 CPS data indicated that sixteen to twenty-four year olds accounted for 28 percent of national employment in establishments with fewer than twenty-five workers and 24 percent of the employees in establishments with twenty-five to ninety-nine employees, but only 18 percent of the workers in establishments with five-hundred or more employees. *See* Report of the President, *The State of Small Business*, (Washington, D.C.: U.S. Government Printing Office, 1986).

84. Of all non-enrolled seventeen-to-twenty year old civilians in March 1988, including those with one or more years of post-secondary schooling, approximately 35 percent did not possess a high school diploma and 8 percent had completed one or more years of post-secondary schooling. In comparison, 56 percent of the poor lacked a high school diploma or GED, and only 3 percent had completed at least one year of post-secondary schooling.

85. Marcia Freedman, "The Youth Labor Market," *From School to Work: Improving the Transition* (Washington, D.C.: U.S. Government Printing Office, 1976, pp. 21–36); Stephen F. Hamilton, "Work and Maturity: Occupational Socialization of Non-College Youth in the United States and West Germany," *Research in the Sociology of Education and Socialization* 7 (1987): 287–312; Paul Osterman, "An Empirical Study of Labor Market Segmentation," *Industrial and Labor Relations Review* 28 (July 1975): 508–521; and Osterman, *Getting Started*.

86. Sum, Taggart, Fogg, *Withered Dreams*; Sum and Fogg, *Labor Market Turbulence*.

87. Sum and Fogg, *Labor Market Turbulence*; Sum and Fogg, *Changing Economic Fortunes*. ·

88. The real median weekly earnings (in 1967 dollars) of eighteen to twenty-four year old women employed full time in 1987 were 17 percent below that earned by identically-aged women in May 1973. *See* Earl F. Mellor, "New Household Statistics on Weekly Earnings," *Employment and Earnings*, October 1980; U.S. Department of Labor, Bureau of Labor Statistics, *Employment and Earnings*, January 1988.

89. Rachel Friedberg, Kevin Lang, and William T. Dickens, "The Changing Structure of the Female Labor Market, 1976–1984," *Proceedings of the Forty-First Annual Meeting* (Industrial Relations Research Association Series, Madison, WI, 1989, pp. 117–124).

90. Given the relatively low number of poor young adults with some post-secondary schooling, the labor force and employment position of non-enrolled poor young adults with twelve or fewer years of schooling were examined in more detail. Our definition of "non-enrolled" in Chart 22 was based on the major activity of the respondent during the reference week of the survey. Those citing "school" as their major activity were classified as students while all others were considered to be non-enrolled. This less rigorous definition of enrollment was necessary to make the 1973 and 1987 findings compatible. Starting in 1986, the monthly CPS questionnaire contains a set of questions that identifies the actual school enrollment status of all sixteen to twenty-four year-olds.

91. U.S. Bureau of the Census, 1989.

92. Employed young men and women from poverty households tend to be substantially under-represented in durable manufacturing, wholesale trade, finance/insurance, and public administration industries relative to their counterparts from higher income households. Employed young males from poverty households were only half as likely as their counterparts with household incomes three or more times above the poverty line to occupy jobs in the above industries and employed, young women were only one-fourth as likely to do so.

93. Richard M. Cyert and David C. Mowry, eds., *Technology and Employment* (Washington, D.C.: National Academy Press, 1987); Lisa M. Lynch, "Race and Gender Differences in Private-Sector Training for Young Workers," *Proceedings of the Forty-Fifth Annual Meetings* (Industrial Relations Research Associa-

tion, Madison, WI, 1989, pp. 557–566); Sum and Fogg, *Labor Market Turbulence.*

94. Clifford Johnson and Andrew M. Sum, *Declining Earnings of Young Men: Their Impact on Poverty, Adolescent Pregnancy, and Family Formation* (Children's Defense Fund, Washington, D.C., 1987); Sum, Taggart, Fogg, *Withered Dreams.*

95. Paul O. Flaim and Nicholas I. Peters, "Usual Weekly Earnings of American Workers," *The Monthly Labor Review*, March 1972, pp. 28–38.

96. Richard B. Freeman and David A. Wise, eds., *The Youth Labor Market Problem: It's Nature, Causes and Consequences* (National Bureau of Economic Research, Chicago, IL: University of Chicago Press, 1982); Richard B. Freeman and Harry J. Holzer, "Young Blacks and Jobs-What We Now Know," *The Public Interest* 78 (Winter 1985): 18–31; Mellor, "New Household Survey," pp. 7–13.

97. The Consumer Price Index for All Urban Consumers (CPI-U) was used to convert 1982 nominal earnings into their 1988 dollar equivalents.

98. U.S. Bureau of Labor Statistics, 1989.

99. Median weekly earnings estimates are available for only one-fourth of the sample each month. The estimate includes both part-time and full-time employed.

100. Robert J. Blendon, "What Should Be Done About The Uninsured Poor?," *Journal of the American Medical Association* 260 (December 2, 1988): 3276–77; Vincente Navarro, "A National Health Program is Necessary," *Challenge*, May/June 1989, pp. 36–40.

101. Our analysis of the March 1988 CPS public use tape revealed that 15 percent of adult males lacked any form of health insurance coverage during calendar year 1987. Coverage rates rise continuously by age group, with 88 percent of thirty-five to fifty-four year olds having some form of health insurance coverage and nearly 100 percent of those sixty-five and over being covered. *See* Clifford Johnson, Andrew M. Sum, and James Weill, *Vanishing Dreams: The Growing Economic Plight of America's Young Families* (Children's Defense Fund, Washington, D.C., 1988); Sum and Fogg, *Labor Market Turbulence.*

102. Forty-three percent of poor young women (age twenty to twenty-four) received health benefits under Medicaid, while only 17 percent of poor young men did so.

103. The findings on health insurance and pension coverage pertain to the situation of respondents in a given calendar year. The unionization questions are based on the status of employed respondents at the time of the survey. The CPS asks these questions on union membership/collective bargaining coverage for only one-fourth of the sample each month.

104. Richard B. Freeman and James L. Medoff, *What Do Unions Do?* (New York: Basic Books, 1986).

105. Peter Doeringer and Michael J. Piore, *Internal Labor Markets and Manpower Analysis* (Lexington, MA: D.C. Heath, 1971); Richard Edwards, Michael Reich, and David Gordon, *Segmented Work, Divided Workers: The*

Historical Transformation of Labor in the United States (Cambridge, England: Cambridge University Press, 1982).

106. Dale Belman and Paula B. Voos, "Race and Labor Market Segmentation Among Women Workers," *Industrial Relations Research Association Series, Proceedings of the Forty-First Annual Meeting*, (Industrial Relations Research Association, Madison, WI, 1989); William T. Dickens and Kevin Lang, "Testing Dual Labor Market Theory: A Reconsideration of the Evidence," (NBER Working paper, Cambridge, MA, 1985); Paul Osterman, "An Empirical Study of Labor Market Segmentation," *Industrial and Labor Relations Review* 28 (July 1975): 508–521.

107. Richard S. Belous, "Contingent Workers and Equal Employment Opportunity," *Industrial Relations Research Association Series, Proceedings of the Forty-First Annual Meeting*, Madison, WI, 1989; Richard S. Belous, *The Contingent Economy: The Growth of the Temporary, Part-Time and Subcontracted Workforce* (National Planning Association, Washington, D.C., 1989).

108. Johnson and Sum, *Declining Earnings*; Mercer L. Sullivan, "Absent Fathers in the Inner City," *The Ghetto Underclass: Social Science Perspectives, The Annals*, vol. 501 (Newbury Park, CA: Sage Publications, January 1989, pp. 48–58); Mark Testa, et. al., "Unemployment and Marriage Among Inner-City Fathers," *The Ghetto Underclass: Social Science Perspectives, The Annals*, vol. 501 (Newbury Park, CA: Sage Publications, January 1989); William Julius Wilson, *The Truly Disadvantaged: The Inner City, The Underclass and Public Policy* (Chicago, IL: The University of Chicago Press, 1987).

109. Berlin and Sum, *Towards a More Perfect Union*; Anthony P. Carnevale and Janet W. Johnston, *Training America: Strategies for the Nation* (The American Society for Training and Development and National Center on Education and the Economy, Alexandria, VA, 1989).

110. The debate over the issue of "poor workers versus poor jobs" has been an on-going one for the past two decades. *See* Doeringer and Piore, *Internal Labor Markets*; Eli Ginzberg, *Good Jobs, Bad Jobs, No Jobs* (Cambridge, MA: Harvard University Press, 1979); Bennett Harrison and Andrew M. Sum, "Data Requirements for Dual or Segmented Labor Market Research," *Concepts and Data Needs* (National Commission on Employment and Unemployment Statistics, Washington, D.C.: U.S. Government Printing Office, 1980); Michael L. Wachter, "Primary and Secondary Labor Markets: A Critique of the Dual Approach," *Brookings Papers on Economic Activity*, vol. 3, 1974.

111. The availability of new training arrangements and the organization of work are likely to be related, but further research is clearly needed. *See* Phyllis A. Wallace, "Training: Maintaining the Competitive Edge," *Industrial Relations Research Association Series, Proceedings of the Forty-First Annual Meeting* (Industrial Relations Research Association, Madison, WI, 1988).

112. The previous New Careers programs were designed to create new para-professional positions in public and non-profit organizations and to develop new career ladders for entry-level workers.

113. Other public policy efforts to improve the economic rewards from

work include the Earned Income Tax Credit and child care subsidies to working low income parents. These policies are designed to supplement the after tax or disposable incomes from work. *See* David T. Ellwood, *Poor Support: Poverty in the American Family* (New York, NY: Basic Books, Inc., 1988); Johnson, Sum, and Weill, *Vanishing Dreams.*

THE HIGH-STAKES CHALLENGE OF PROGRAMS FOR ADOLESCENT MOTHERS

Judith S. Musick

"When I was about 11 or 12 I was very lonely, so then I went to having sex and then I got pregnant and that was my way of curing my loneliness (by) having kids. That's the best thing I have in this world and that's my kids."[1]

From the journal of an adolescent mother

A FOURTEEN YEAR OLD RUNS AWAY from home, and in spite of involvement in various youth service programs, repeatedly involves herself in self-destructive relationships. Through ongoing crises, these eventually lead her to far more serious troubles.

A sixteen year-old mother drops out of school, and then abandons her counselling and GED[2] programs. Later, she appears to lose job after job, and have baby after baby, "deliberately."

When such personal failures take place, it is not simply that the environment has offered these adolescents few realistic or appropriate options. It is not just that the institutions in the community are not particularly sensitive or responsive to their needs. Certainly, there are numerous real obstacles in the way, in any direction they turn; but, there are sometimes opportunities as well—people who want to help, chances to start again. These go unheeded or unused.

Basically, many such teens do not perceive or trust people to be sources of help. For others, the psychological burdens of their histories lead them to put their trust in the wrong people, those who will

The material in this chapter is derived from the author's book on the psychology of adolescent motherhood, forthcoming from Yale University Press. The work was supported by grants from the Rockefeller and Harris Foundations.

111

hold them back, or who will betray them again and again. People who cannot be trusted, or who are trusted but betray them, fit easily into these girls' working models of themselves. Such people are seen to fill familiar roles and to serve functions similar to people the girls have come to know so well.

This chapter is focused on a group of adolescent girls who have experienced the serious problems of a developmentally damaging childhood, and on how they respond to the challenges and changes of the adolescent years. Although diverse in many ways, the members of this group generally have qualities in common—poverty, and vulnerability to early childbearing. Overwhelmingly, it is poor girls who have children while they are still adolescents.

The chapter will describe how certain experiences associated with disadvantage disrupt the developmental process, creating pathways that lead young women, even those with considerable promise, to premature parenthood and unfulfilled potential. The purpose in raising these developmental issues is twofold: first, to set the stage for a more meaningful and ultimately more useful discussion of early childbearing and its attendant problems in the domains of school, work, and interpersonal relationships; and, second, to provide a framework for considering how current strategies for preventing or ameliorating problems such as adolescent childbearing mesh with the facts of underlying psychological dynamics—that is, to ask how well our externally constructed "solutions" match the internal realities of the problems.

ADOLESCENCE, DEVELOPMENT AND THE PROCESS OF CHANGE

"My father really hurt me emotionally very bad. . . . That's why I spent so much time at my boyfriend's house and then I got pregnant."

"Now to my mother. I hate her so much. She has never been a mother to me. I hate her to my heart. My mother used to treat me like dirt. That's why I had a baby. So I can show the best possible love towards my baby than anyone has ever given me."

From journals of adolescent mothers

The attitudes and values a family holds, and the support and guidance the family context provides, help to determine how adolescence will be experienced by a son or daughter. At this critical developmental juncture in life, a parents' attitudes, values, support, and guidance take on great significance, particularly within an environment fraught with risks. While certain adolescent difficulties arise from developmental psychopathology, others emanate from the particular attitudes, values, and ideas held by the girl's family, peers or community.

Not surprisingly, the most serious, most intractable difficulties are the result of interactions among these motivational root systems. A discussion of these interactions is critical to understanding both risk and prospects for "recovery," because it highlights those conditions that tend to foster repeated unwise choices, as well as those conditions which enable people to change. Say, for example, that a disadvantaged girl has been raised in a loving and supportive home, but one in which a high school diploma is viewed as an end in itself, rather than as a launching pad for further achievements. This girl may lack direction or be less likely to seek and work towards college or career goals, but once exposed to previously unthought of possibilities and given adequate time, guidance, emotional, and perhaps material support to make them realities, she may well embrace new goals, and seek the knowledge and experiences required to reach them. She is open to opportunity; she is, or can be, motivated to change.

On the other hand, what if an adolescent's lack of direction stems not just from her family's notions about high school being an end in itself, but also from their mistreatment and neglect of her emotional needs, or from their ignoring, discounting or disparaging any accomplishments which threaten to make her different or better than they are? Such an upbringing is unlikely to engender the considerable willpower, perseverance, and sense of purpose it takes to stick with and master new knowledge, skills, and ways of interacting, especially in a community environment which offers so few supports to its youth.

In this instance, there is a different and more complex set of motivations at work, one which is more deeply rooted and thus more resistant to change. The adolescent with this kind of personal history must do more than just take on new attitudes about education and work, she must also acquire and internalize new ways of thinking and feeling about herself and others—new, and often quite different, ways of interacting with people and institutions. Unfortunately, an adolescent from such a home is often without the critical underlying motivations for change, *since such an upbringing also makes change, even objectively very positive change, a subjectively risky endeavor.*

Motivations underlying the ability to envision a future, to make reasonable, self-enhancing choices about moving towards it, and to see and seize opportunities, are not "givens." They do not automatically unfold within the human psyche. Rather, they are psychological skills acquired only under certain conditions, developmental accomplishments predicated on the existence of essential familial and societal lessons and supports.

Optimally, these are available when the child, and later the adolescent, is most ready for them, when developmental readiness is prime. At present, we do not know if or under what circumstances, one can *learn* (or be taught) as an adolescent motivations or psychological skills which should have been acquired as a child. Unfortunately, the personal histories of many disadvantaged adolescents are made up of just those conditions which make the providing of these lessons and supports least likely to occur.

PSYCHO-SOCIAL ROOTS OF EARLY PREGNANCY

Too-early childbearing is one of the most common psychological "products" of poverty's multiple ill effects on developing young people, effects that reach into the heart of families to reduce their capacities to provide average, or "good enough," child-rearing environments.[3] Severe poverty contributes to conditions in which children's development can be thwarted, blocking their paths to success in school and diminishing their capacities for healthy, self-enhancing interpersonal relationships.

A developmentally poor start, in turn, frequently prepares the ground for early motherhood by encumbering girls with the kinds of psychological burdens that, within the context of disadvantage, lead to self-limiting choices and self-defeating behaviors during the adolescent years. And, unlike their "mainstream" sisters, when disadvantaged girls make bad choices, or engage in risky behaviors, they are likely to be closing doors which can never be reopened. Those who come of age in poverty are given very little margin for error in negotiating the tasks of adolescence.

In the process of trying to cope with the challenges of adolescence in poverty—of seeking to resolve "normal" developmental issues in contexts where "normal" options and models are scarce, and where pressures to engage in risky behaviors are plentiful—many girls become mothers while still in their early teens. Developmental-environmental interactions are the wellsprings of this early parenthood. Understanding this fact is necessary to an understanding of why adolescent childbearing and the problems associated with it are such psychologically robust phenomena, so deeply rooted in the individual, and so strongly resistant to change. The severely problematic attitudes and values of poor teens reflect troubled developmental histories; their mistaken "choices" grow out of unmet developmental needs.

Many such choices have serious negative consequences for the adolescents' lives; many of their unmade decisions result in pain and failure that is so extreme that it inevitably generates a new round in the cycle of poverty. Nevertheless, for the adolescent the actions make psychological sense at that moment. They feel right because they promise to spare her the greater turmoil and disequilibrium she would experience were she to behave differently. While such self-destructive or self-defeating behaviors may appear puzzling to outsiders who observe them, they seem logical and fitting to the adolescent, since they are the natural outcomes of her personal history and sense of self as these interact with the day-to-day realities of her life.

SIXTEEN IN THE MAINSTREAM: STRUGGLES, AND SUPPORTS

Annie Dillard, the Pulitzer Prize-winning writer, describes her emotionally stormy adolescence in her memoir, *An American Childhood*:

> "When I was fifteen, I felt it coming; now I was sixteen, and it hit. My feet had imperceptibly been set on a new path, a fast path into a long tunnel. . . . I wandered witlessly forward and found myself going down. . . . There wasn't a whole lot I could do about it, or about anything. I was going to hell in a handcart, that was all, and I knew it and everyone around me knew it, and there it was. I was growing and thinning, as if pulled. I was getting angry, as if pushed. . . . My feelings deepened and lingered. The swift moods of early childhood—each formed by and suited to its occasion—vanished. Now feelings lasted so long they left stains. They arose from nowhere, like winds or waves, and battered at me or engulfed me."[4]

Raised in the 1940s by a strong, loving (and well-to-do) two-parent family rooted in the past and current life of their community, Dillard made mistakes, and took risks, but the foolishness of her adolescence could be weathered, and its experiences successfully integrated as part of her developing self, without pulling her down forever.

Most adults in society's mainstream recognize that adolescence is a major crossroads, that time of life when a young person's future life-course begins to be set in earnest. As Lawrence Steinberg points out in "The Logic of Adolescence" in this volume, "adolescence is a period of preparation, defined less by its own essence than by what it is followed by—maturity." The process of achieving maturity has its own particular challenges in current U.S. society, but as he notes, it is a process that most adolescents undergo with reasonable success. For most mainstream adolescent girls, entry into the period of adolescence takes place against a backdrop of psychic strength and integration, gained from the successful execution of the basic developmental tasks of childhood.[5] Even as identity is being re-tested and re-formed during adolescence, and the building of adult relational skills and practical competence is undertaken, there is normally a core of emotional and intellectual "wholeness" working for the individual.

In addition, however, there are likely to be numerous parental and other social supports to help the adolescent overcome her problems. Too much turbulence, or too little achievement, is taken seriously by at least some of those observing the teenager's behavior. For example, parents and teachers alike are likely to be concerned when a formerly motivated girl seems suddenly to lose interest, or to fail in school. The significant adults in such a girl's life will recognize that for some reason she is currently unable to handle the varied pressures of adolescence, unable to balance its often conflicting internal and external pulls.

Adults will be concerned when a girl acts out sexually, perhaps in response to problems, such as the loss of a father or family discord, which leave her without the emotional support and guidance she needs to cope with her unfolding sexuality. It is believed to portend problems in future relationships (e.g., marital relationships) if a girl attempts to resolve identity conflicts by involving herself with a series of "Mr. Wrongs."

When parents are not able or willing to help, a good quality school, with caring, involved teachers and guidance counselors can be lifesaving (literally, as well as symbolically) for an adolescent who is troubled or in crisis. As an external support system, a good school can serve as a model, encouraging and reinforcing an adolescent's coping efforts, and demonstrating positive values.[6] Those who have studied stress resistance in adolescence find that resilient adolescents usually have extensive contacts outside their immediate families. These contacts include concerned and caring teachers, as well as ministers, and older friends.[7]

A "mainstream" girl whose sexual acting-out results in a pregnancy will probably have an abortion. If her religion forbids this, she will be far more likely to relinquish her child for adoption than will her disadvantaged counterpart.[8] In those comparatively rare cases where a girl from a "mainstream" economic background does elect to keep and raise her baby, she has a greater chance to marry than does her disadvantaged counterpart; has greater material resources; and, even if she is a high school drop-out, she has a greater likelihood of eventually getting a job through her family or their connections in the community. As difficult and potentially damaging as adolescent developmental tribulations can be—in particular for girls, the tribulations associated with sexuality—they are far less likely to have lasting negative effects.

Thus, for most mainstream girls, temporary psychological vulnerability need not inevitably result in permanent disability. For the travails of a troubled youth, there are the cushions and buffers of a relatively stable social and economic environment. As with girls like Annie Dillard, a "wasted" or troubled youth does not automatically lead to a wasted life.

SIXTEEN AND POOR: A DIFFERENT EXPERIENCE; A DIFFERENT IDENTITY

For many adolescent girls who have been raised in an environment of severe poverty, reality is different in virtually every dimension. These girls frequently have grown up in damaged and damaging family situations, in which the basic developmental foundation of childhood has been poorly laid or—in the case of some key elements—perhaps is not there at all. In addition, the environment in which such girls live, at home, in school and in the community, is often highly threatening. At the same time, external supports are few, and are generally inadequate.

"I grew up with two alcoholic parents that's a bad start. I have 3 brothers who cared for mom and fought off Dad—one of my babysitters made me sleep with her son. I had my first b-friend at 11 he was 22. I guess I needed a father figure well I didn't stop there I always had older boyfriends. I'm remembering now I never knew how to say "no." Don't ask how I kept my virginity but somehow I managed to get in and out of relationships never going all the way. Meanwhile my Mom'd get drunk every weekend and my Dad was messing up too. My brothers left one by one forcefully getting married. I stayed home and took care of my mom. When my parents got a divorce my Mom got worse if that's possible. I got crazy. I got into a gang when I was 12. I got drunk with friends tried a joint and came home at 1:00 am. At 13 I was getting bad grades going into 7th grade my Mom quite (sic) drinking I quite (sic) messing up. Well I graduated a honor student and got into Brooks.[9] At this time I knew everything about guys and how not to get myself into trouble by looking to fall in love. My Freshy year I got bad again cause I cared more about having fun. Soph year I met Bob the father of my son. I fell in-love and wasted my virginity on him. I got pregnant and was lost alone and confused. Lucky I found God. I have my son now and I have a new life."

From the journal of an adolescent mother

What happens to the teenage girl in the world of poverty who flounders when confronted with the challenges of the adolescent "passage," who engages in sexual acting-out, who finds and involves herself with males who exploit or abuse her, or who fails in school? More often than not, she is drawn into a vortex from which there may be little chance of escape, either up or out.

The difficulties that face such a young woman on a regular basis can range from overt daily threats of random and unpredictable violence, to subtle but ubiquitous pressures to engage in risky sexual behavior. She is constantly at risk of giving up on making something of herself, or on envisioning and working towards a better life for her future. Beyond that, however, there is frequently a deeper problem. The transformations in relations with family, peers and the community that generally accompany adolescence are being handled by these girls quite differently in very important respects.

Based on what we know, for example, about typical "mainstream," adolescent girls, we see them struggling to come to grips with the following questions: "Who am I? What are these feelings I'm feeling? Do my parents understand me? Are they listening to me? What do they know? I'm old enough, why won't they let me do what I want? What should I do about my sexual attractiveness to boys? How do I feel about sex? How do I balance my social and school lives? And, especially in the mid- to later- adolescent years, will I go to college? If so, where? What will I do with my life—will I have a career, or marry and raise children, or both?"[10]

On the other hand, many of the girls who come of age in "under-class" communities—especially, those in single-parent, father-absent families, are struggling with different questions. They too are asking "Who am I?," but from a psychological perspective that belongs to an earlier period of development.[11] For these girls, the "Who am I?" issues, the issues of *identity*, often are not predominantly those of redefining and renegotiating family relationships, searching for a sense of where one is headed in the future, and envisioning the place one will take in the broader society. Rather, identity-related issues may still be grounded in the questions of early childhood: Who cares about me? Who can I trust? Who can I depend on? Where and how can I find security and safety?

"I like it when people notice I'm having a baby. It gives me a good feeling inside and makes me feel important."

From the journal of an adolescent mother

The self's voice in these young women articulates one basic set of questions: "What do I need to do, and who do I need to be, to find someone who will stay close to me, and care for me like I wish my mother (or father) had done? What do I need to do, and who do I need to be, to find a man who won't abandon me, like the men in my life and my mother's life have done?"

If an adolescent's psychological "wholeness" is fundamentally compromised, much of her time and effort will be focused on trying to resolve her unmet dependency needs, searching for and trying to maintain attachments, in a defensive, security-oriented manner. When this occurs, her attention and her energies are diverted from the critical developmental tasks that undergird adolescent, and later, adult competence in our society. Girls for whom basic acceptance and love are *the* primary motivating forces have little interest or emotional energy to invest in school or work-related activities, unless they are exceptionally bright or talented in some area. Even then, the pull of unmet affiliative or dependency needs may be more powerful than anything the worlds of school or work have to offer, particularly when these offerings are as inadequate and inconsistent as those found in most poverty communities.

FIGHTING THE ODDS

The adolescent girls most likely to be struggling with the developmental tasks that really belong to childhood are those who have been forced to adapt to family and other environments which provide too little care and protection for their children and youth. In searching for the acceptance and love they crave, these girls will take many risks and few precautions. The capacity for self-care is, after all, predicated on a history of being cared for and protected by others. While growth-thwarting personal histories are by no means exclusive to impoverished communities, they are more predominant there for a variety of reasons, and their effects are far more lethal within that context.[12]

"I'm going to tell you about my suffering. When I was 5 years old I had to go and stay with an aunt. She was very bad with me, and then I had to go to another aunt and she was even worse. . . . one day my mother appeared and picked us up. It's not fair that you have to be going from place to place even if it's with your family, and it's bad when somebody from your family doesn't have pitty (sic) on you. Like you didn't have the same blood, but that happened to me. They did not have pitty on me. They did not care for me. They did not defend me. I was so small I could not defend myself against adults. I had suffered since I was a small child. I always ask myself how come God gave me this punishment. What had I done to deserve all this suffering. . . . Sometimes you have to be weary (sic) of even your brothers and sisters, uncles and aunts, and especially about stepfathers. Some of them are very tricky, you should never trust a stepfather that is not good to you, I can say this because I had (it) happen, he lived with my mother. Even though they lived with my mother doesn't mean I have to love them as my father, because even sometimes we can not even trust our own fathers, I never met mine so I don't know what it is to have a father, but I know about step-fathers because I have had them. . . . some of them take advantage of you and even in the same family they do things like that. They resemble animals that don't even respect their own family."

From the journal of an adolescent mother

"When I was small I got so many disappointments with friends and families that it is hard to trust some one again. . . . When I was small I don't know why but I was scared of big people most likely adults. Today I feel afraid like if someone is chasing me or something is going to happen to me. I usually have these awful feeling (sic) I wish I could take it away because it feels terrible and it is very uncomfortable to live with it. I hope I can make it disappear someday."

From the journal of an adolescent mother

Abusive or neglectful experiences in childhood do much more than foster bad attitudes and actions; they act to shape an inadequate adolescent sense of self and identity, one which prohibits forward movement in positive, self-enhancing ways, even when "opportunities" present themselves. Such life experiences in early childhood and in the years immediately preceding adolescence leave girls developmentally unprepared for the rapid and extensive physical and psychosocial changes of the adolescent period. For these girls, there is little or no foundation for resisting the internal and external pressures of the teen years. These pressures find them psychologically unprepared, overwhelm their psyches and "pull the rug out from under them" emotionally.

For girls as well as boys, life in an impoverished environment can begin with a neglecting or abusive mother, one for whom drug addiction or other self-destructive behavior may be overwhelming. An inadequately developed teenager herself, she may be totally unable to give her children any real nurturing care. Particularly for the daughters of such mothers, an additional kind of abuse—sexual victimization—can be a frequent occurrence.

This childhood experience is far from uncommon in the personal histories of many adolescent mothers.[13]

"I learned about sex from my dad. I never had a chance for my first time with my boyfriend. Who knows, maybe I would have wanted to wait until I got married. But no, I never got to have that chance. I don't even remember the first time. . . . it ruined my life."

"I learned about sex by being molested (by) friends and a couple of family members. . . . I sometimes think I have a sex drive cause I was molested so many times as a child."

"My experiences and memories of sex wasn't too good. It was ugly and violent and I will never forget."

From journals of adolescent mothers

A girl learns about truth and trust initially as a very young, dependent child, from the ways she is or is not protected from daily harm. If, in addition to inadequate basic care, she is also subjected to sexual abuse, it teaches highly damaging lessons that go beyond issues of sexuality. When a girl learns about sex through coercion, trickery, seduction or violence, she learns perverse lessons about the giving and getting of affection; about what she means and is worth to others. If she is abused early, or often, she can also learn shame, fear, guilt, and silence, and how to keep herself from knowing what is simply too painful to bear.

When the first sexual lessons a girl learns shape her sexuality in developmentally inappropriate ways, the experience is destined to have far-reaching negative implications for how she perceives the world and lives her life. The interpersonal context in which her sexual socialization takes place affects much more than her sexual behavior *per se*—more, even, than her relationships with males. Because it can affect her deepest sense of who she is and what she can do, it also can reduce or even demolish her capacity to care for and do for herself, to conceptualize and control her own destiny. In critical ways, of course, it will also damage or destroy her capacity to care for her children, or to direct their destinies in positive ways as parents are supposed to do.

Thus, for a severely disadvantaged girl, inappropriate, exploitive sexual socialization is often the last and heaviest "straw" in a mounting accumulation of damage. When its effects are combined with those of fatherlessness and other interpersonal deprivations, she becomes highly vulnerable in relation to males. If, in addition, she does poorly in school—as her psychic damage makes likely—she will find herself without the requisite skills for success in the wider world. Thus she is left without the inner strength, confidence, or capacity that comes through mastery in domains beyond the interpersonal. For such a young woman, the interpersonal is all there is.

In a broader context, her social isolation as a member of an "underclass" community frequently administers the psychological *coup de grace*.[14] Lack of sustained contact with or exposure to mainstream people and institutions "fixes" interpersonally dysfunctional ways of relating, and seems to help weaken the functional boundaries that normally exist between the personal and other aspects of one's life. The interaction of psychological and social deprivations helps to insure that the lives of many poor adolescent girls will be virtually ruled by a pathological and over-dependent dysfunctional relationship to men not just in the bed or on the street, but in the classroom, factory or office; not just as a female, but as a student, worker, and parent as well.

The childhood experience of sexual victimization, even more than other forms of abuse, thus takes a heavy toll on development, affecting intellectual, as well as social-emotional functions. Most importantly, it seems in many cases to leave a psychological residue of emotional discontinuities—breaks between present and past, between thought and feeling, and between actions and intentions.[15] When this happens, the girl is functionally the prisoner of the disavowed and unacknowledged pain of her past.[16] Emotional discontinuities cause her to be caught between the security-seeking behavior that experience has taught her to engage in and want, on the one hand, and the security-threatening results of that behavior, on the other. She cannot easily "learn" from these repeated "mistakes," because the feelings and perceptions are not related to each other. As a matter of psychic self-protection, she has developed a pattern of compartmentalizing, so that what appears to her as functional (even "rational") survival-oriented behavior is not psychically related to its invariably negative outcomes. She has "learned" to perceive her participation in abusive interactions that cannot be avoided as, in effect, a positive skill, and in so doing, has come to insulate her emotions from the normally associated pain.

Thus the stage has been set for a series of personal crises, crises that the girl herself has (either actively or passively) instigated, but about which she appears to be bewildered. "How did this happen to me?" "How did I get pregnant?" "How did I get kicked out of school?" "How did I lose the job? I didn't do anything wrong." "How did I get involved with a (another) guy who takes advantage of me, who beats me up?" "How did I get involved with a man who abuses my kids?" "Why did the state take my kids away?"

Laurie: "You know I always wonder why us teenagers always pick the same guy."

Interviewer: "What do you mean, 'pick the same guy'?"

Laurie: "Well when you are getting out of a relationship, then you fall in love with the same kind of guy. We pick almost the same guy all over again. I don't understand how I got from one bad circumstance to another. I could have prevented the second one. I was working, going to school, doing fine and then I was careless and ignorant. I didn't take birth control that weekend I got pregnant. There was no reason for this, I had the information in my hand, I thought it's not going to happen to me, I'm not going to have sex. I was trying to deny the fact that it was me, my ignorance."

From an interview with an adolescent mother

". . . . for girls, I think they don't give a care if they are alive because they got sexually abused and they will go around just jumping into any other guys bed. . . . after it happens they feel so cheap and fleezy and they don't care about their life anymore. . . . 'they are hurting me so why shouldn't I hurt myself?' They don't care. 'Why should I care?' So they will go out and you know ruin their life more."

From the journal of an adolescent mother

For those who question why an adolescent, even one who is in an intervention program, continues to seek and find more trouble, or is at best able to go only so far, it is important to remember that such patterns of behavior are usually grounded in what are unfortunately necessary, perhaps even life-saving, adaptations to terrible life circumstances.

Because such adaptations initially (and repeatedly) "worked," they are deeply ingrained in self and identity, and thus strongly resistant to change. Few of the young women who exhibit this syndrome as participants in intervention programs could be said to be mentally ill, or even to have severe personality or character disorders. Indeed, many have remarkable strengths and resilience.[17] Still, seriously and continuously depriving experiences are rarely without psychological consequences. These, in turn, interfere with the ability to negotiate the critical tasks of this adolescent transitional period, and, in circular fashion, create additional vulnerabilities that magnify the effects of risk factors in the environment. When this happens, the adolescent is left without the personal resources and coping skills she most needs to withstand the multiple pressures of her daily life, or to thrust herself up and out of poverty. It is fate's cruel trick that in order to move beyond a life of poverty, today's disadvantaged adolescent needs to possess not just good, but extraordinary psychosocial resources and skills; not just an adequate self concept, but one which is virtually invincible.

How does an eleven-year-old girl handle her changing body and her emerging sexuality in a home where she is nightly faced with her own young mother's active sexual life with a series of temporary live-in lovers? How does she make sense of these psychological and physical changes within the context of her own sexual exploitation at the hands of these men, or other older males within her family environment? What do such failures of parental protection do to the mother-child relationship at a developmental period when the girl has a heightened need for her parent's support and guidance? How will this girl relate to her peers and to potential boyfriends? What will be their particular meaning in her life? What functions will they need to fulfill for her?

During adolescence, girls in healthier family environments are in the process of transforming their earlier, more dependent relationships with their parents, while continuing to feel a need for their support and guidance. What happens to that girl who must distance herself emotionally from her family in order to survive? What compensatory psychological benefits can such girls obtain from putting their energies into doing well in school? Where will they find the psychic "energy" to invest in school, considering what they are trying to cope with in relation to their families, friends, and perhaps boy-friends?[18] How do such emotional burdens interact with the educational limitations conferred by their early life experiences in their homes and in the less than adequate schools of their communities? What kinds of messages do such experiences impart to the girl about who she is? How do they affect her images and concepts about her self? What additional power might a girl's peer group have when it needs to fulfill roles and functions that her parents are unable or unwilling to carry out?[19]

The psychological consequences of growing up in potentially growth-thwarting milieus are not the same for all adolescents of course: some are stronger and more resilient than others.[20] Neverthe-less, in an environment of risk, even relatively minor developmental damage can create vulnerabilities which diminish the ability to sense and actively avoid dangerous or risky situations and behavior, and in such environments danger and risk are the order of the day.

Developmental damage will interfere with the young woman's later capacity for competent functioning in the broader, or mainstream society. This is especially true when such damage is compounded or exacerbated by attitudes, ideas or values prevalent in her community—drug or alcohol abuse, lack of identification with mainstream culture, an acceptance of welfare dependence, a defeatism about job prospects, a comfort with sexual or other "misbehavior"—that can lead even a very healthy and resilient girl into trouble, can keep her from realizing her potential, and can block her capacity to make use of help to change.

So it is that the adolescent females about whom our society is currently most worried, the ones who are sliding (or actively propelling themselves) towards futures of disorganization, dysfunction, and dependence, are coming of age without a core of preparatory experiences essential for success in our rapidly changing society, a society which increasingly requires its members to be literate, flexibly able to acquire and deploy new skills, and above all, interpersonally deft. Those who seek to interrupt disadvantaged adolescents' self-defeating patterns of behavior, or to deflect their downward trajectories, are frequently puzzled by what appears to be their stubborn resistance to mainstream ideas and values; by their continuing to take risks, and appearing to make ruinous personal choices; and, worst of all, by their refusal to take advantage of the chance to acquire or use new knowledge and skills. As we have seen, this behavior is not so puzzling when its antecedents are understood.

INTERVENTION AND PREVENTION

In spite of the formidable challenges involved in changing a troubled life, and in averting a downward spiral, there is hope. The girl is, after all still an adolescent. While it appears that maximum opportunity for malleability of self-structures occurs during the earliest years of life,[21] the transformational nature of the adolescent process probably opens the door to positive change wider than it may ever be opened again. Because she is still experiencing broad developmental evolution, is still young, and is in significant ways still relatively flexible, her potential for change is at a peak. Being an adolescent certainly means that in some ways she is at greater risk, but in other ways it also offers a priceless opportunity for change. In a sense the adolescent's "weakness" is also her strength. Developmental transitions automatically bring with them a breaking down of some earlier structures and new chances to make something of oneself. Such chances do not come again very easily or frequently after the psychologically integrating experience of adolescence is completed. And, if one result of this integration is, in effect, a death of the "spirit," later interventions may be useless for all practical purposes.

Just as good youths can "go bad" at this time, "bad" youths can "go good" under the right circumstances. But, what are the right circumstances? Are they to be found in the current programs aimed at troubled or at-risk adolescents in communities across the country? Considering the powerful developmental and psychological factors underlying adolescent parenthood and its accompanying problems, considering the external pressures that exist and the opportunities that don't, isn't it time to reconsider the nature of our interventions? Can we honestly say that they match the nature of the problems?

> Counselor: "Just as Carrie was on the brink of making some positive personal and educational changes, she seemed to *deliberately* stop herself from succeeding by getting pregnant again. I'd have to say that Maria accomplished much the same thing by dropping out of the (young parent support program) right after we notified her that she had been accepted in a really exceptional job training project. Lisa "forgot" to take the entrance exam for a special junior college program, and Ginny took her twin sons out of the day care program that was enabling her to finish high school. After going 'round and round' with us about how bad he was for her, Donna went back to the boyfriend who beats her up, and who practically keeps her a prisoner in the house."[22]

Why did these young women apparently sabotage themselves? Didn't they recognize or want these opportunities? Didn't they welcome changes for the better? These are questions we ask each time we are confronted with a "failure at the moment of potential growth."[23] Such failures are not exceptions, they are common occurrences—sources of frustration and bitter disappointment for teachers, guidance counselors, health care and social workers, "big sisters," home visitors, ministers, and others involved with adolescents at risk. These failures at moments of potential growth come at the point in an adolescent's life where her personal history and contemporary pressures interact negatively with what is being offered by supportive others from outside her family and peer networks.

It is the psychological and developmental aspects of this interaction that best predict the direction, degree, and timing of any positive movement on her part. Just as such personal factors are implicated in her current troubles, they are implicated in her response to efforts to overcome them.

Whenever an adolescent girl begins to experience the desire for positive change, whenever she musters the will to make it happen, it is because of a shift not only in the external contingencies of her life, but just as significantly, in her internal self-concepts as well. For poor adolescents, as with all adolescents, such shifts can come about only when developmental readiness meshes with realistic opportunities to succeed in *personally valued* roles and areas of competence; when opportunities are coupled with support and positive regard from *psychologically meaningful* others; when there are concomitant *shifts in self-image and self-regard*; when the *new (or future) identity* required is *not too discrepant* from the present one; and, when the *psychological costs* do not *outweigh the benefits* to the self.

In order for a program or policy to have a meaningful impact on the psychological factors that lead a girl to become a mother while still an adolescent, it must in some way alter her identity and other self-concepts, her internal representations of herself. Whenever an intervention is effective with a particular teen, whenever it helps her to feel and be more competent, to better understand what motivates her actions; to *think* before she automatically does something; and, whenever it helps to bring about a shift in her values or behaviors, it is at least partially the result of the intervention's "fit" with her own developmental needs and psychological makeup.

Perhaps for all people, but certainly for those adolescents drawn to early childbearing, *positive change is most likely to occur within the context of strong and repeated emotionally salient experiences, with personally significant people.* The need for the positive sanction and caring of an important other is *the* fundamental need for young women with developmentally damaged psyches.

> "(The program). . . . is a place to open up. To learn more about yourself. If you have a good group facilitator, the questions that are put towards you make you think. It was a place to let out tension that was going on in the family during the day, you could come discuss it with someone. . . . *Here is where I got my start.*[24] In helping at the office and becoming more sure of myself it caused me to think my problems through and not just act."

> "I was really depressed cause I thought I wasn't going to achieve anything, and then I came and talked to Ms. Bowen and the others that works here and they influenced me to go back to school."

> "She helped me with, well I was going through some emotional

changes and so the times that I couldn't make it they would visit and talk with me and comfort me in some way. . . . They were a big influence on that, they stayed on me and on me about finishing school. . . . I could have been out on the streets, young girl pregnant you know, just at home on welfare you know, but they showed me I could be more than that, I could be a lot more than that. . . . I see that I can be anything I want to be and still take care of my baby. . . . They picked up my pieces, even put them back together and showed me I'm a person. Life is not that bad and it's not that hard, just give it a chance. . . . Confidence, don't talk about confidence, I didn't have any. My confidence was gone."

"I keep coming here because you help me to think."

Comments from adolescent mothers[25]

If we seek to facilitate positive change in adolescents, particularly when such change requires thinking and acting in ways that are radically different from those of the most significant people in their lives, the supposed benefits of such change will have to be both developmentally appropriate and powerfully motivating on an individual psychological level. If they are not, they stand virtually no chance of altering downward trajectories. To be so motivating, interventions must reach and touch young people at the level of the self, that deepest and most strongly felt sense of who one is.

Although one hears, from policymakers and others concerned with the interaction of adolescent childbearing and poverty, a good deal of rhetoric about the "complexity of the problems" and about the need for more "comprehensive" interventions for at risk youth, few have been willing to grapple with the psychological and developmental aspects of that complexity. Failing to remember that these young people are adolescents, they fail to understand that key developmental purposes are being served by engagement in early sexual activity and parenthood. It is precisely because such fundamental needs are being addressed—however unsuccessfully—in too-early parenting that leads it to occur in spite of all argument and apparent reason. If such needs could be met in more functional, self-enhancing ways, they would be. That is the psychological meaning of having "few options."

Those concerned with youth at risk and with the kind of programs that might help them only infrequently take account of what comprehensive intervention strategies might actually entail in terms of the interactive relationships between adolescent development and interventions,[26] especially as these in turn influence and are influenced by other significant relationships in the girl's life. The fact is, for the average disadvantaged adolescent girl, to choose actively *not* to have a child is symbolically to "do it better" than all of the emotionally significant people in her life—with virtually no material, educational/ vocational or emotional supports for doing so.

Just think of what that takes! If a parent does not (or cannot) actively enable a child to go where she herself has gone or beyond—does not consistently tell the child that she wants and expects her to succeed, and does not show her how, the child can rarely do so. Poor adolescents who succeed in spite of the fact that they live in environments of failure generally have more than skills and strengths, they have extraordinary families who act as buffers and enablers;[27] and, sadly, sometimes even these families cannot keep their daughters from early parenthood.[28]

That some very bright and promising poor girls from loving families also have babies too early is powerful testimony to the strength of the forces promoting and surrounding premature motherhood where there are few meaningful social alternatives. When these forces interact with the teen's developmentally normal desire to fill adult-like roles, to be a "woman," and with aspects of her social environment that encourage or at least do not condemn teenage parenthood,[29] you have to wonder, under these circumstances, who wouldn't have a baby?

The adolescent girls who face the most severe problems of developmental disadvantage will not change simply through disembodied efforts to help them feel better about themselves, through programs to "enhance self-esteem."[30] Authentic self-esteem rests on the mastery of valued and valuable skills, on becoming somebody who really can do something. Conversely, simply providing greater educational or vocational "opportunities" will not motivate change if these opportunities are not provided in the context of enabling and, if need be, healing relationships. In fact, without such relationships, most won't even be perceived as opportunities, merely as unwanted and thus unheeded pressures to change.

A change in life course for a severely disadvantaged adolescent is likely to call for emotionally risky transformations in relationships between herself and family members, friends, boyfriends, and other significant adult figures. Such changes may take place within a range of contexts, but all are strongly interpersonal in nature. Thus, in addition to the need to develop, master, and deploy new cognitive capacities and behavioral skills, to hold and begin to live by different attitudes and values, the young adolescent woman will often need to alter certain powerful, affectively-charged relationships that are at the emotional center of her life.

"I know that if I want to make something of myself, I'm going to have to leave him."

From an interview with an adolescent mother

But it won't be easy. Having sex and having children are relational behaviors. Since many problems in these domains stem from relational problems in the family, it is through relationships that they are ultimately remedied. But, relationships are only the starting points, the instruments: they are the vehicles to help adolescents develop masteries in skill and social areas—real life, valuable skills *and* new ways of interacting. And not just any relationships will do, but special kinds of relationships, with special people—people whom the adolescent perceives as similar, wishes to be like, or wishes to impress. For *adolescents*, (adults are a different issue) educational or social programs, whatever their aims or institutional bases, must be places ". . . . where order, purpose, pride and love prevail."[31] The scaffolding relationships for building new skills can only be found within such contexts.

Just as poor adolescents need better than good families to move up and out of poverty, they need better than good schools, social programs, and other opportunities. In truth, however, it is the rare school, social program, skills or job training setting for disadvantaged youth that provides important and supportive relationships *consistently*, over a *sufficient period of time*, to *sufficient numbers* of teens to have a noticeable, let alone significant, impact. [32]

More often than not, the programs and educational opportunities for disadvantaged young people are as disorganized and unpredictable as the homes so many of them grew up in. Because they rarely expose disadvantaged adolescents to positive social networks for sustained periods of time (if at all), they compound physical isolation. Because direct service and teaching are frequently provided by staff who are undertrained (and in some instances barely one step ahead of the teens themselves), they inadvertently compound social and educational isolation.

It is a hard truth, but few of us can help others to go beyond where we ourselves have gone, to find and make use of opportunities we have not made use of ourselves.[33] The roads that lead out of poverty must be laid and maintained by skilled professionals, as well as community-based staff. Disadvantaged adolescents need repeated exposure to "outside" (that is, mainstream) ends and means. They need exemplary programs offering positive alternative role models, and skilled, as well as caring, mentors and teachers. The importance of well-trained teachers and program staff cannot be overstressed.

". . . . for children who are used to thinking of themselves as stupid or not worth talking to or deserving rape and beatings, a good teacher can provide an astonishing revelation. A good teacher can give a child at least a chance to feel 'she thinks I'm worth something. Maybe I am.' Good teachers put snags in the river of children passing by, and over the years, they redirect hundreds of lives."[34]

This refers to teachers, but it could equally well be said of any caring person in any teaching, mentoring, or therapeutic role: That is what effective interventions do: put "snags"—life-saving, rescuing snags—in the river of adolescence. Because so few people have been trained for this very special and demanding kind of youth work, it can be done only for "hundreds," not for the thousands upon thousands of adolescents who are deeply troubled, or at high risk of becoming so. Obviously, more funding would be necessary in order to reach greater numbers of adolescents, but it will never be sufficient without a new cadre of adolescent specialists or youth workers with broader knowledge (and heightened sensibilities) about the psychological and developmental as well as social and economic determinants of adolescent behavior. The time is long overdue for *well-organized* efforts to recruit and train such workers.

It is also time to shine a light on those educational, health, and social strategies that we already know are effective; emphasizing (and *re*emphasizing) that they currently reach only a fraction of those in need, and taking a hard look at the barriers to implementing them on a larger scale. While each life saved is always of consequence, the greater the number of changed lives the higher the chance that positive effects will spill over to affect larger groups and "systems" of adolescents.

Ultimately though, psychosocial interventions will count for little in the absence of realistic opportunities for disadvantaged young people to become participating members of society. In order for disadvantaged adolescents to do it differently, to do it better, *both* the psychological and social conditions of their lives, and the economic realities, must be altered. Psychological change without something real to strive for is no more functional by itself than is a "wonderful job" that the adolescent is not emotionally, socially or educationally prepared for. It is the weaving together of both strands that counts. A school or social program can and should serve as a bridge to the wider world, but the adolescent must believe there is something on the other side of the bridge that is worth crossing for. If she does not, she will turn back and refuse to cross it.

Finally, there are two related but poorly understood issues that thwart efforts to ameliorate or prevent the problems of adolescents growing up in poverty.

First, intervention—that is, remediation or amelioration—is what we find ourselves doing when serious risk or problems already exist. Prevention is of a somewhat different order. Although in some cases the two may overlap, in others they are likely to be quite separate, just as what one does to *cure* a disease is frequently quite different from what is done to *prevent* its occurrence. Growing up self-assured and competent is always better than having to struggle to become so at a later date. Naturally-occurring family support and enablement are always better than their socially (and artificially) constructed analogs.

Second, at its best, *selective intervention* cannot possibly reach and help every troubled young person; perhaps in the end it can only help those who are also strongly motivated or who have considerable untapped potential.[35] Unfortunately, we are still unclear about how to create the conditions which constitute *general prevention*; those which will promote optimal growth for all children. For instance, it is often remarked that waiting until adolescence is too late for pregnancy prevention, and that a special emphasis must be given to reaching youth in the junior high school years.[36] But, what do we really know about the conditions for lasting positive change in the pubertal or early adolescent periods? Very little indeed. Junior high schoolers are very heterogenous in terms of physical and social-emotional maturity. Is earlier always better? What about the significance of the middle and adolescent periods in relation to the human capacity for transformation of self? We had better be careful that we do not faddishly, to say nothing of precipitously, give up on adolescents. Americans seem all too willing to shift with the prevailing winds when it comes to complex problems that fail to respond to simple solutions.

NOTES

1. Throughout this chapter, quotations appear that are taken from journals written by adolescent mothers, as part of a program of intervention designed to help them protect their children and themselves from sexual exploitation (Heart-to-Heart).

An important strategy for reaching this goal is to encourage these young women, especially those who have been sexually victimized as children and/or adolescents, to reflect on their own sexual histories and present and past relationships with men. Since some girls would find it too uncomfortable to engage in such self-reflection within a regular group format, a decision was made to make journal writing an integral part of Heart-to-Heart.

2. General Educational Development Certificates, a high school diploma equivalent.

3. The concept of the "good enough" childrearing environment is derived from the late British psychoanalyst D.W. Winnicott's notion of the "good enough" mother. *See* B. Bettelheim, *A Good Enough Parent: A Book on Child-Rearing* (New York: Knopf, 1987). Bettelheim has extended this concept to include two parents, since both are significant for their child's development. The concept suggests that it is possible for parents to raise their child well, even though they are far from perfect. Mistakes in rearing one's child are, in this framework, more than compensated for by the many instances in which the parent does right by the child. *See also* U. Bronfenbrenner, "Ecology of the Family as a Context for Human Development Research Perspectives," *Developmental Psychology* 22 (1986); 723–742 and J. Garbarino, *Children and Families in the Social Environment* (New York: Aldine, 1982). The notion of good enough parenting could well be extended to include the total ecology of childrearing as conceptualized by Bronfenbrenner and Garbarino. In this case, threats to development arising from one sector of the environment, e.g. the family, may be mitigated by compensatory factors in the other people and institutions to which the young person is exposed. Conversely, the effects of noxious or highly stressful community conditions may be buffered by an exceptionally strong and nurturing family life. Of course, such notions assume an intact organism. If this is not the case, even greater compensatory mechanisms will be called for. See, for example, the transactional model of A. Sameroff and M. Chandler, "Reproductive Risk and the Continuum of Caretaking Casualty," F.D. Horowitz, *et. al.*, eds., *Review of Child Development Research* 4 (1975): 187–244.

4. A. Dillard, *An American Childhood* (New York: Harper and Row, 1987), 222.

5. J. Garbarino, "Early Intervention in Cognitive Development As a Strategy for Reducing Poverty," in *Giving Children a Chance: The Case For More Effective National Policies*, ed. G. Miller (Washington, D.C.: Center for National Policy Press, 1989).

6. M. Rutter, *et al.*, *Fifteen Thousand Hours: Secondary Schools and Their Effects on Children* (Cambridge: Harvard University Press, 1979).

7. S. Hauser, and M.K. Bowlds, "Stress, Coping and Adaptation Within Adolescence: Diversity and Resilience," in *At the Threshold: The Developing Adolescent*, eds. S. Feldman and G. Elliott (Cambridge: Harvard University Press, 1990); E. Werner and R. Smith, *Vulnerable But Invincible: A Study of Resilient Children* (New York: McGraw-Hill, 1982).

8. J. Musick, A. Handler and K. Waddill, "Teens and Adoption: A Pregnancy Resolution Alternative?" *Young Children* 13 (1984): 24–29; C. Hayes, ed., *Risking the Future: Adolescent Sexuality, Pregnancy and Childbearing* 1, National Academy of Sciences (Washington, D.C.: National Academy Press, 1987).

9. A good public high school which requires entrance examinations, and is selective about who is admitted.

10. Some of the best and most recent sources of information on "normal" adolescent development can be found in the recent volume on that subject commissioned by the Carnegie Council on Adolescent Development. This volume, was edited by Shirley Feldman and Glen Elliott (see note 7). Professor Feldman generously provided copies of chapters in progress; they were invaluable for this work. Appreciation is also due to Dr. Ruby Takanishi of the Carnegie Council for information about the book, and for a referral to Professor Feldman.

11. Ironically, some behaviors, such as early sexual relations and parenthood, appear to be more "grown-up." See L. Steinberg, this volume.

12. R. Halpern's work on the Child Survival/Fair Start initiative, "Community-Based Early Interventions," in S. Meisels and J. Shonkoff, eds., *Handbook of Early Intervention* (Cambridge, MA: Cambridge University Press, 1990, pp. 469–498); W. J. Wilson, *The Truly Disadvantaged: The Inner City, the Underclass and Public Policy* (Chicago: University of Chicago Press, 1987); D. Ellwood, *Poor Support: Poverty in the American Family* (New York: Basic Books, 1988). These all provide a sense of the cumulative effects of poverty on the family. Halpern deals more with family functioning—specifically, parenting—whereas Wilson and Ellwood are more concerned with structural issues such as family formation. The specific family and other environmental experiences which are most toxic for pre-adolescent and adolescent girls are examined in depth in the author's forthcoming book on the developmental and psychological dimensions of adolescent childbearing, particularly as these relate to positive personal change.

13. H. Gershenson, J. Musick, *et. al*, "The Prevelence of Coercive Sexual Experience Among Teenage Mothers," *Journal of Interpersonal Violence* 4(2) (1989): 204–219. In a recent study they found that over 60 percent of their sample of 445 pregnant and parenting adolescents had been sexually molested in their childhood, preteen and early teen years (mean age of first abuse = 11.6 years). Of this group 65 percent had been abused by multiple abusers and/or on multiple occasions. Only 2 percent of the perpetrators were strangers, most being members of the girls' kin or near-kin networks.

14. The term "social isolation" refers principally to phenomena described under this heading by Wilson in *The Truly Disadvantaged*.

15. Mental health professionals refer to such "discontinuities" as forms of *dissociation*, psychological defenses used to retain a sense of self under traumatic or brutalizing conditions.

16. Obviously, unhappy childhoods thwart the development of male as well as female children. See R. Taylor's chapter in this volume for a discussion of adolescent males; see D. Cicchetti and V. Carlson, eds., *Child Maltreatment: Theory and Research on the Causes and Consequences of Child Abuse and Neglect* (Cambridge: Cambridge University Press, 1989), particularly the chapter by M. Rutter, for descriptions of how a history of parental maltreatment affects behaviors and choices made in adolescence and early adulthood; see also the volume on sexual abuse, by J. Haugaard and N. Reppucci, *The Sexual Abuse of Children* (San Francisco: Jossey-Bass,1988), particularly chapter 4 on consequences for victims.

17. The Ounce of Prevention Fund's 40 prevention/early intervention programs serve approximately 3,500 girls each year. About 1,500 of these girls are in junior high school programs aimed at preventing adolescent childbearing. Thus they are not already pregnant or parenting. Although few are seriously disturbed, it is important to remember that the girls who are "together" enough to attend these community-based education and support programs are generally not the very poorest functioning adolescents. Few programs have been able to engage the latter girls for any significant period of time, if at all.

18. See for example, E. Anderson, "Sex Codes and Family Life Among Poor Inner-City Youths," *ANNALS, AAPSS* 501 (January 1989): 59–78 on the powerful forces of male ghetto street culture which support and even encourage early sexual activity and teen pregnancy.

19. J. Bily and J.R. Udry, "The Effects of Age and Pubertal Development on Adolescent Sexual Behavior." (Unpublished manuscript, 1983, cited in *National Research Council*, 1987); G. Cvetkovich and B. Grote, "Psychological Development and the Social Program of Teenage Illegitimacy," C. Chilman, ed., *Adolescent Pregnancy and Childbearing: Findings From Research* (Washington, D.C.: U.S. Department of Health and Human Services, 1980). In general, girls have been found to be more likely to be swayed than boys by the actual or presumed sexual behavior of their peers, especially their best friends and their boyfriends. It should be noted however, that peer influences are less compelling among African American samples, with white girls being more susceptible to peer influences than their African American counterparts.

20. N. Garmazy, "Stressors of Childhood," in N. Garmazy and M. Rutter, eds., *Stress, Coping and Development in Children* (New York: McGraw-Hill, 1983, 43–84); N. Garmazy, A. Masten and A. Tellegen, "The Study of Stress and Competence in Children: Building Blocks for Developmental Psychopathology," *Child Development* 55 (1984): 97–111; N. Garmazy, "Stress, Competence and Development: Continuities in the Study of Schizophrenic Adults, Children Vulnerable to Psychopathology, and the Search for Stress Resistant Children," *American Journal of Orthopsychiatry* 57 (1987): 159–174 on children vulnerable to psychopathology. *See also* The work of M. Rutter, "Resilience in the Face of Adversity: Protective Factors and Resistance to Psychiatric Disorder," *British Journal of Psychiatry* 147 (1985): 598–611 and "Psychosocial Resilience and Protective Mechanisms," *American Journal of Orthopsychiatry* 57 (1987): 316–331 on resilience in the face of adversity; E. Werner, on the "Vulnerable but Invincible" children of Kauai, in E. Werner and R. Smith, *Kauai's Children Come of Age* (Honolulu: University of Hawaii Press, 1977); E. Werner and R. Smith, *Vulnerable But Invincible: A Study of Resilient Children* (New York: McGraw-Hill, 1982); E. Werner, "High Risk Children in Young Adulthood: A Longitudinal Study From Birth to 32 Years," *American Journal of Orthopsychiatry* 59 (1989): 72–81. All of these authors present striking evidence of the remarkable coping and adaptational abilities of many children raised in environments of risk. A careful reading of their findings, however, indicates that even for the most resilient young people there are often serious, albeit more subtle costs.

21. J. Bowlby, *Attachment and Loss* 3 (New York: Basic Books, 1980).

22. These examples were derived from extensive clinical material, case notes and observations gathered over a six-year period.

23. J. Musick, "The Psychological and Developmental Dimensions of Adolescent Pregnancy and Parenting: An Interventionist's Perspective." Paper prepared for the Rockefeller Foundation, December, 1987.

24. Author's underlining.

25. Thanks to Dr. Jeannie Gutierrez of the Erikson Institute for clinical case material.

26. The phrase "interactive relationship between adolescent development and intervention" comes from a discussion several years ago with R. Selman of Harvard University's Judge Baker Clinic. It nicely captures what should be happening in community-based programs for youth and adolescents, but which so seldom does.

27. See, for example, Reginald Clark's, *Family Life and School Achievement: Why Poor Black Children Succeed or Fail* (Chicago: University of Chicago Press, 1983); or James Comer's story of his own family, *Maggie's American Dream: The Life and Times of a Black Family* (New York: New American Library, 1988).

28. These daughters do tend to be more motivated to move ahead in positive ways, to seek and make good use of help. They also seem better able to avoid getting caught up in the pattern of rapid, repeated childbearing that characterizes teens from more troubled families.

29. The journalist Leon Dash has written a thought-provoking book titled, *When Children Want Children: The Urban Crisis of Teenage Childbearing* (New York: Wm. Morrow, 1989). He sees the lingering aspects of the rural, sharecropping past as continuing to promote early parenthood in today's urban settings where it has far outlived its original purpose.

30. In her comprehensive review of interventions to prevent adolescent high risk behaviors, J. Dryfoos found that "affective programs that tried to raise self-esteem and make young people 'feel better' about themselves were not successful in any of the fields." Indeed, she makes the case, confirmed by the observation discussed in this chapter, that no single solution works. J. Dryfoos, *Adolescents at Risk: Prevalence and Prevention* (New York: Oxford University Press, 1990).

31. This is how the scholar E. Gordan describes his own strong family upbringing in "Ordinary Black Women," a review (with Cynthia Grace and Brenda Allen) in *Readings: A Journal of Reviews and Commentary in Mental Health* 2 (New York: American Orthopsychiatric Associations, 1989), 12–17

32. In *Within Our Reach: Breaking the Cycle of Disadvantage*, New York: Anchor, 1988, L. Schorr points out that small, demonstration programs, with outstanding, professional or professionally-supervised staff, tend to lose their potency (and thus their efficacy) once they move from the demonstration phase to large scale replications. See also Musick and Halpern (1989) for a discussion of this issue in regard to the early childhood period. J. Musick and R. Halpern, "Giving Children a Chance: What Role Early Parenting Interventions,"in *Giving Children a Chance: The Case for More Effective National Policies*, ed., G. Miller (Washington, D.C.: The Center for National Policy, 1989).

33. J. Musick and F. Stott, "Paraprofessionals, Parenting and Child Development: Understanding the Problems and Seeking Solutions," *Handbook of Early Intervention*, ed. S. Meisels and J. Shonkoff (New York: Cambridge University Press, 1990), 651–667.

34. T. Kidder, *Among Schoolchildren* (Boston: Houghton Mifflin, 1989), 313.

35. Let there be no mistake, it is crucial to help such adolescents. Many who seek and *use help* would not be able to make it on their own, and would fall back into the ways of their less gifted peers. The pressures are simply too great.

36. It does seem clear that, as J. Dryfoos states in *Adolescents at Risk*, a (if not *the*) major focus of prevention and intervention initiatives should be the schools, since low achievement is a major risk factor for virtually every high risk behavior of youths. In addition to the acquisition of basic skills, schools can and should be the locus for other non-academic preventative interventions because that is where virtually all children (and to some extent their parents) can be reached, at least in the earlier school years.

POVERTY AND ADOLESCENT BLACK MALES: THE SUBCULTURE OF DISENGAGEMENT

Ronald L. Taylor

A RECENT ANALYSIS OF THE STATUS of youth in American society concluded that a search for structure—that is, for a meaningful and attainable set of expectations and standards to facilitate self-definition and guide the transition from child to adult status—is a dominant feature of the experiences and behavior of youths from a diversity of backgrounds and regions of the country.[1] This study argues that, until quite recently, the institutional contexts of family, school, media, workplace, peer group, and the criminal justice system interacted to produce a code of rules which most youth internalized as a guide to behavior and as a frame of reference for interpreting experiences. To the extent that these institutional contexts were in relative harmony with one another, they provided a coherent structure and sense of direction for adolescents, organizing the transition from childhood to the assumption of adult roles. With an increasing disharmony and disequilibrium coming to characterize the network of social institutions charged with the responsibility for socialization of the young in many communities, however, adolescents have come more and more frequently to internalize disharmony and confusion in their psychosocial organization.

In such a context, many youths, particularly poor youths, are left "to chart their own course or, much worse, to pick a route from among the often confusing signals put out by the family, the peer group, the school, and the work place."[2] The result is often a growing sense of futility, disaffection and resistance to any formal structure. Nowhere is the frustrating search for structure, consistent guidance, and support more evident in the United States than among black youths in the inner-cities. Their communities have been ravaged by unrelenting poverty, high rates of unemployment, and a host of other social ills which have undermined or eroded the authority of those social institutions traditionally charged with the intimate socialization of black children and youths.

Three elements of the overall disintegration of inner-city social structure have been most significant, and most destructive in terms of socialization. Structural shifts in the economy (i.e., the shift from manufacturing to service industries as a source of employment growth), it has been argued, may be, "the single largest force behind the increasing social and economic marginality of large numbers of inner-city blacks," creating "a set of mutually reinforcing spatial and industrial changes in the country's urban political economy that have converged to undermine the material foundations of the traditional ghetto."[3] Among these structural shifts is the decentralization and relocation of industrial plants from the urban core to the suburbs and abroad, contributing to the precipitous decline in the number of jobs available to inner-city blacks in primary labor markets.[4]

The deterioration in the inner-city economy, in turn, has been associated with negative social changes in black communities, such as the rise in number and proportion of households headed by single females, and in the proportion of black youths concentrated in the inner-cities.

Finally, the exodus in record numbers of working and middle-class black families has removed to a significant degree the "social buffer" they once constituted against the advance of various forms of social dislocation. Such families provided "much of the fine texture of organizations and patterned activities that allowed previous generations of urban blacks to sustain family, community and collectivity even in the face of continued economic hardship and unflinching racial subordination."[5]

In sum, the increasing social and spatial concentration of poverty in the inner-cities of this country, and the growing predominance of social ills long associated with such poverty—family disruption, school failure, drugs, violent crime, housing deterioration, etc.—have quantitatively and qualitatively altered the psychosocial as well as the material foundations of life for most of the inhabitants, intensifying the conditions of economic marginality and social isolation.

For a large and growing number of inner-city youths, therefore, the ability to adjust to recent changes in the economy and in the community has been overwhelmed by the magnitude and intensity of such changes. In response to a disappearing local economy, disintegrating community institutions, social isolation, and spatial concentration, a *subculture of disengagement* from the wider society appears to be surfacing among some segments of inner-city youths.[6]

The tendency toward progressive disengagement from the norms and values of the larger society is not a phenomenon unique to black inner-city youths; it can be observed also among poor white and Hispanic youths whose linkages to family, education, and economic institutions are weak or unstable.[7] It has its origins in the limited opportunity structure and growing disarray of the socialization framework encountered by black and other poor and minority adolescents. But the influence of the subculture of disengagement is most broad-spread and most pernicious for black children in general, and black males in particular. Its impact is reflected in the dramatic rise in youth gangs and violent behavior, and in soaring rates of out-of-wedlock births, drug use and abuse, and school failure.[8]

An increasingly important factor contributing to the problem, particularly among black males, is the paucity of positive role models with whom they can identify and from whom they can acquire the knowledge, guidance, values, and skills so essential for positive identity development and a sense of direction. As one recent study of middle-class and low-income black male adolescents revealed,[9] a sense of self-determination, confidence in the future, and willingness to explore alternative possibilities for self-actualization and achievement can be related directly to strong role model identification (or lack thereof). For low-income inner-city males, the relative lack of significant role model identification was associated with, among other things, a lack of confidence and trust in their social environment, as well as their perception or experience of restricted alternatives or opportunities for assuming responsible adult roles in mainstream society. As a result, many of these youths perceived no meaningful "pay-offs" between role model identification and their immediate or long-term goals and aspirations.

The discontinuity and conflict in relationships among the various socializing environments to which black adolescents are exposed can be illuminated by examining the nature of their experiences in the family, school, peer group, and larger community. Given the nature and quality of their interactions in these contexts, poor black male adolescents tend to experience even more difficulties than their female counterparts in reconciling the contradictory values, expectations, and demands of their environments and in negotiating the difficult transition to adulthood, more often drifting toward delinquency, crime, drugs, and other forms of antisocial behavior.[10]

This chapter examines the experience of black adolescent males in economically deprived and psychologically hostile environments, where many are forced to take refuge in peer group and other activities which offer opportunities for positive self-definition and support but which also often imbue attitudes and values contrary to long-term interests and well-being.

Experiences in the family, are examined first, experiences which serve to structure much of the relationship with other social environments. Next, the school experiences of these youth are discussed, along with some implications of these experiences for other realms. Subsequent sections review the role of peer groups as sources of emotional support, status, and self-direction, and the ways in which prior experiences in the home, in school, and on the streets influence black male adolescents' orientations toward their adult social worlds.

BLACK FAMILIES, SOCIALIZATION, AND MALE ADAPTATIONS TO INNER-CITY LIFE

As society's basic institution, the family assumes major, if not exclusive, responsibility for early socialization, furnishing the child with an initial milieu and shaping the child's view of the social world. Most parents bring to the task a body of knowledge, beliefs, values, and skills fairly well suited to ensuring that children will develop a repertoire of interactive and other behavioral skills appropriate to doing well in the environment in which they live. The knowledge, beliefs, values, and skills parents seek to pass on to their children are not parental inventions; they are the products of the collective experience of past and current generations. The socialization agenda and child rearing practices of families and other agents of socialization vary, however, with the nature and requirements of the social environment, as well as with the degree of access families have to the economic system in which they are embedded.[11] Thus, in negotiating their socio-cultural environments and in exploring the opportunity structure available to them, different populations evolve "different strategies appropriate to the respective environments and these strategies determine to a large degree the repertoire of instrumental competence—physical skills, cognitive skills, communicative skills, social-emotional skills, etc.—characteristic of members of each population."[12]

More specifically, in most societies, stratified as they are on the basis of criteria which result in differential access to economic opportunity and resources, such differences tend to create different imperatives. Depending upon the nature of the close-in world a child is born into, different skills and behaviors will be required, ones appropriate to the specific environment for both children and adults. Given the nature of the effective environment of poor inner-city black families, characterized by severely limited opportunities for participation in conventional economic activities, marginal family and community resources, and minimal life chances for social mobility, it should not be surprising that the formulas such families employ in socializing their children to survive and prosper in such an environment differ from and often actually contradict the formulas employed by families living under "mainstream" environmental circumstances.

It is essential to emphasize the importance of the environment within which the socialization of poor black children takes place, and the manner in which the ecological pressures inherent in that environment dictate the choice of child rearing techniques or practices, as well as the skills and behavior to be acquired. Much research on black families and black childhood socialization has tended to take out of context child rearing practices and resulting child behavior, separating it from the realities of life in the inner-city.[13] This has fostered the misleading impression that child rearing practices in such families are irrational or random activities, whereas in fact they are part of a culturally organized system which has evolved to meet environmental demands.[14]

Black children in the inner-cities, like other children, experience a variety of family structures and living arrangements, and these offer varying degrees of support, protection, and emotional security during the early years of development. Some grow up in two-parent families, others in extended and augmented families. The majority, however, now grow up in single-parent female-headed households, in which the mother's boyfriend may frequently or occasionally reside. Although single-parent households are often associated with a number of social, psychological, and economic disadvantages for children, many such families can be just as effective as other families in raising children to become competent, responsible, and well-adjusted adults.[15] But, single-parent households in the inner-city encounter enormous difficulties in meeting the material and emotional needs of their children and in protecting them from the harsh realities of ghetto life. Moreover, such difficulties are exacerbated in households headed by single teenage mothers, who are forced to assume adult responsibilities for the support and care of children long before they are capable of handling them.[16]

In preparing their children to survive the dangers and hardships of life in the ghetto, black parents place great emphasis on early independence and self-reliance.[17] The development of these attributes in children is facilitated by sharp decreases in individual attention and nurturance as they grow older, by physical punishment and verbal sanctions, and by the assignment to the child of various tasks and responsibilities usually carried out by adults in other families. Such techniques are not indicative of parental rejection of children; rather, they reflect a desire to instill a capacity for functional and emotional independence, in an environment which offers limited opportunities to be dependent upon adults. In consequence, children tend to grow up fast in the inner-city, and develop characteristics and skills which equip many of them to survive the unrelenting series of harsh experiences to which they are exposed.[18] As the authors of one study of the children of Harlem observed in reporting their results, such children:

> "learn early that life is often unkind and that pain and suffering are a very real and unavoidable part of the human condition. They tended to develop the strength required to adjust to a life demanding early self-reliance, with minimal emotional support. They learned how to cope with a variety of people and situations on their own, with little protection from adults. They became increasingly hardened to physical punishment. All of these adaptations may be viewed as strengths because they enhanced the children's chances for survival in a society that is hostile to them."[19]

During infancy and early childhood, there is little evidence of differential socialization by gender among black families in the inner-city. On the contrary, parents appear to instill in both male and female children similar traits of independence, assertiveness, and self-reliance.[20] However, as children reach school age, differential treatment and parental expectations by sex become more apparent. It seems that mothers tend to focus on and anticipate the difficulties girls are expected to encounter as they assume the responsibilities of motherhood and strive to keep their families together in the face of severely limited resources and support. Mothers, therefore, are likely to invest more time and other resources in training their daughters for self-reliance and independence than they invest in their sons, whom they often assume can make it more easily on their own.[21] As one researcher succinctly put it, poor black mothers "raise their daughters and love their sons."[22] Thus, from an early age, black females tend to be given more emotional support than males, which may help to explain why female adolescents are more resistent to peer pressure and influence than are black males.[23]

The burden of rearing children without a husband to share the responsibilities for discipline and guidance may partly account for the limited investment mothers are able to make in the rearing of their sons. This, in combination with their forlorn sense that boys will inevitably get into trouble of one sort or another, or are destined to be claimed by the triple menace of drugs, mayhem or murder (given their greater exposure to the dangers of the streets), may have the effect of lowering their expectations for their sons, and lessening their willingness to invest in their sons' upbringing.

Though boys often are subjected to harsher punishment because their mothers are attempting to control their behavior and protect them from the lure and dangers of the street, such punitive treatment more often than not causes suppressed anger, anxiety, and mistrustful attitudes toward adults, as well as increasing defiance of parental authority.[24] And since boys tend to receive less emotional support as they grow older, they may conclude that they have relatively little to lose in failing to regulate their behavior in accordance with parental demands and directives. Thus a common complaint of poor black parents—especially mothers—is their inability to exercise control over their children, especially boys, and the growing involvement of their youngsters in the peer group and culture of the streets.[25]

The absence of fathers from inner-city families, both as role models and as disciplinarians for their sons, is undoubtedly a major factor in the loss of control over them, and helps to account in part for their dependence on peer groups as a source of the solace and direction that are relatively unavailable at home.[26] In fact, father-absence is associated with a number of the social and psychosocial developmental problems experienced by black male youths, particularly poor youths. Father-absence is significantly related to differences in academic achievement between black boys and girls, with the academic performance of the latter less affected by father-absence than the former.[27] Likewise, the absence of fathers as role models has been shown to impair positive identity formation among black male adolescents.[28]

But even where fathers are present in the home, the nature of their interactions with their sons may be such as to render them unattractive as models. Sons whose relationship with their fathers is characterized by their fathers' distant, cold, quarrelsome, and punitive behavior, and who perceive their fathers as lacking in the ability to provide resources in support of the family, will be inclined to reject them as significant others or to see them as negative role-models in their lives. The tendency among black male adolescents in the inner-city to report no significant role model identification in their lives reflects not only rejection of or ambivalence toward their fathers as creditable role models, but also a general mistrust of adults as objects of strong identification. A lack of trust and confidence in their social environment (a legacy of an often precarious existence), combined with the experience of actual or potential loss of support from significant others, tends to convince these youths that life is capricious and unpredictable, and that adults, including parents, are often "untrustworthy" and "unreliable."[29]

Under conditions of family instability or discord, economic insecurity, and surroundings of chaos, hopelessness, and despair, it is not surprising that adolescents in the inner-city experience great difficulty developing the motivation, competence, and sense of efficacy that culminate in a strong sense of personal identity.[30] While some forge lifestyles that enable them to cope with the anxiety, ambiguity, and the dangers of their environment, others succumb to continuous grief and depression.

THE SCHOOL EXPERIENCE OF ADOLESCENT MALES

Although it is within the family that children initially acquire many of their most important adaptive or maladaptive strategies and defenses for coping with the anxiety, deprivations, and dangers of life in the inner-city, it is within the contexts of the school, peer group, and the wider community that black male adolescents learn the major lessons that shape their lives and program many of them for failure and obsolescence.

The difficulties that black youth in general and black male adolescents in particular experience in the public schools of the inner-city are well documented.[31] Poor black children usually score lower than white children on standardized measures of school achievement, are disproportionately enrolled in the lowest ability groups, and are overrepresented among school dropouts, and among students suspended or expelled from school for misconduct. Moreover, black students, particularly males, are three times as likely to be in classes for the educable mentally retarded as are white students, but only half as likely to be in classes for the gifted or talented.[32]

Although the under-achievement and failure of black children and youth in public schools are often attributed to background characteristics (e.g., family instability, socialization practices, etc.), sub-cultural orientations, and numerous personality and behavioral traits, there is considerable evidence that their poor performance in school is more often a function of the quality and character of public schools.[33] It has been argued that, through their structure, policies, and social relationships, public schools in poor communities are often vehicles for promoting a hidden agenda and curriculum for poor children and youth which, in conjunction with other social institutions, collaborate in the maintenance of poverty, inequality, and deprivation of black and other minority children.[34]

To be sure, certain attitudes, behaviors, and cultural orientations of black children in the inner-city are important contributing factors to their under-achievement in school.[35] It has been argued, for example, that because the larger society has for so long denied black Americans access to equal educational opportunities and equal rewards for educational accomplishments, their attitudes toward public schools (though not toward education per se) are often marked by considerable hostility and distrust.[36] Such attitudes, in turn, make it difficult for them to "teach their children effectively, and for the children to acquire the beliefs, values and attitudes that support the educational system and its assumptions and practices."[37] In short, many black children bring to school considerable ambivalence or skepticism regarding their prospects for successful performance in what many of their parents perceive as a hostile and untrustworthy environment. Black children and youth also bring certain cultural orientations and behaviors to the school setting which are often misunderstood, denigrated, or dismissed by teachers and school administrators. Their language, style of interaction and dress, and cognitive approaches to processing information diverge from the cultural conventions and behavioral rules of middle-class oriented public schools, resulting in a lack of cultural synchronization between black students and their teachers.[38]

These background characteristics and orientations interact with the culture and norms of public schools to produce disastrous educational outcomes for many black children. As various studies have shown, public schools that enroll students from lower-class homes tend to adhere to a set of attitudes, policies, and organizational arrangements that have the effect of reinforcing the stereotypical views of such students as incapable and inferior.[39] On the whole, such public schools are more bureaucratic, "are subjected to more rules, have fewer financial resources, have fewer experienced teachers, use a system of rigid tracking, and suspend, expel and discipline (their) students more harshly and more often."[40] In overt and subtle ways, black students are encouraged to adopt attitudes and behavior which predestine them for low-paying, low-status jobs, and inspire feelings of inferiority and low self-esteem. Some students may respond to such expectations by adopting and internalizing them, while others may seek to counter such expectations by refusing to behave in accordance with them. In either case, the results are often the same—poor performance and school failure.

The role of teacher expectations in determining educational outcomes for children is now well-known and extensively documented.[41] In addition to race, class and gender biases have been shown to have major impacts on teacher expectations for student performance.[42] Differential expectations lead to differential treatment of students. Teacher expectations for poor black children are generally lower than their expectations for poor white children, and their expectations for the school performance of black boys are typically lower than for black girls.[43] More often than not, teacher expectations regarding black males are influenced by their stereotype of black males in general, which is frequently characterized by what has been called the five "ds": dumb, deprived, deviant, dangerous, and disturbed.[44] Boys must demonstrate that such characteristics do not pertain to them in order to avoid some of the more severe forms of discipline and debilitating criticism to which many are frequently subjected in inner-city schools. But such stereotypes and prejudices die-hard. As one study found in a longitudinal study of student-teacher interactions in an urban school, teachers often ignore any evidence of students' conduct, abilities, and potential that disconfirms their prejudices and expectations.[45] This finding is of course consistent with standard theories of information processing that tell us how difficult it is for discrepant facts to overcome central assumptions.

The stereotypical views of black males held by teachers, therefore, often act as a self-fulfilling prophesy, whereby the teachers' expectations and beliefs regarding the ability and behavior of black males lead them to behave toward the latter in a manner that inspires as a response the very attitudes and behaviors that confirm the expectations. Thus, for example, because black boys are generally assumed to be more aggressive, hostile, and rebellious than other students, teachers tend to overreact to the misbehavior of these youth by subjecting them to severe disciplinary treatment, ranging from suspension and expulsion to corporal punishment. This in turn can produce either real attitudes of hostility and rebellion, or at least the kind of defiant or resistant behavior usually associated with those attitudes.

Data reported by the Carnegie Corporation and others indicate that black students in general and black males in particular are from two to five times as likely as their white counterparts to be suspended from school at an early age.[46] These data reveal that while minority children represented 25 percent of the national school population in 1983, they constituted 40 percent of all suspended and expelled students in that year. In an analysis of the school suspension records of the elementary, junior high, and high schools of one school district in the Southeast, researchers found that while black students constituted 54 percent of the enrollment, they represented 67 percent of the students suspended at all levels of schooling.[47] For black males, the results were particularly alarming. In this one district alone during one school year, black males at the elementary level missed 159 days of school, in contrast to 62 days for white males, 32 days for black females, and 4 days for white females. Such trends continued at the junior and high school levels, where black boys represented the majority of students who had their education interrupted by suspension.

Most important to an interpretation of these facts is the related finding that black students, and particularly males, are more likely than their white counterparts to be suspended from school for *subjective* offenses reflecting the personal judgments of their teachers, such as disobedience, insubordination, and disrespectful behavior, not just for *objective* offenses such as truancy, fighting, and the possession of drugs or alcohol.[48] Such discriminatory practices undoubtedly contribute to feelings of anger, frustration, and alienation among black students, and to patterns of behavior (e.g., chronic truancy, dropping out of school, etc.) which deter their progress and achievement in school.

In general, research concerning race and gender differences in the quality of school experiences suggests that the relatively poor scholastic performance, negative attitudes, and high attrition rates of black males are at least in part a function of the nature of their interactions and treatment in public schools.[49] One large observational study of teacher-student interactions involving sixty-three classrooms in ten schools located in the Southeast found that, in contrast to other gender-race categories, black males had fewer positive interactions with their teachers, received more negative academic and behavioral feedback, and less unqualified praise and encouragement than other students.[50] The implications of these findings become apparent when viewed in the context of the findings reported in other studies that limited or negative academic feedback to black males is related to the tendency among these adolescents to lower their expectations, downgrade their scholastic abilities, and substitute compensatory terms for positive self-regard and sense of achievement.[51]

Whatever the causes, a series of studies yields several generalizations about black male experiences in public schools.[52] Young black males are:

- more likely to be in the lowest academic tracks,
- more likely to be isolated (socially and academically) from their classmates,

- more likely than white males to be sent to the principal or guidance counselor for challenging the teacher or for other misconduct,
- more likely to be labeled deviant and described in more negative terms by their teachers and other school personnel, and
- more likely to be judged inaccurately by teachers with regards to their general (i.e., global) academic ability.

Consistent with such experiences are the findings that black males have lower school self-esteem (though not general self-esteem or sense of control), and less achievement orientation than other race/gender categories.[53] Given the nature of their experiences in such settings, black boys' negative attitudes toward school, it has been argued, may be seen not only as a cause of their lower attainment, but as a consequence of their mistreatment.[54]

In view of the frequent psychological assaults on their self-esteem black boys experience in school (and often in the home), it is not surprising that they often seek alternative means for validating their self-worth and sense of achievement. Hence, for many inner-city black male adolescents, the peer group becomes the principal means through which they seek both a sense of belongingness and feelings of self-esteem. In fact, for males whose fathers are absent from the home, affiliation with street-based peer groups is a crucial step toward learning many of the socially defined and normative aspects of the male role in the black community and the larger society.

PEER GROUPS AND IDENTITY

Children alienated from their families because of insufficient support, physical abuse, or family discord, and from school because of repeated failure and humiliation, often find the street culture of their peers a welcome relief from the anxiety and stress associated with their other environments. For many inner-city adolescents, both male and female, involvement in peer group culture comes fairly early in life and takes on many of the socialization functions of the family.[55] In one study of black children in Central Harlem, researchers noted the early timing and extensiveness of peer contacts among these children.[56] In combination with some of the difficulties they experienced in their relationships with adults, these contacts influenced the early development of strong peer group affiliations and orientations: "The earlier peer orientation of lower-class children, made possible by the early availability of peer contact, would appear . . . to function in part in a compensatory way as an attempt to secure the nurturance and belongingness that are relatively unavailable at home."[57] Early peer group orientation is also associated with the need for young children in large families to depend upon one another when parental responsibilities are shifted to siblings for care and protection. This "shift in dependency from parents to siblings predisposes children to seek need satisfaction from peers rather than adults at an earlier age than children more extensively nurtured by adults."[58]

Whatever the motivation, early peer group orientation is a common feature of the lives of black children in the inner-city, and such groups play a powerful role in facilitating their development toward adult status.[59] It is largely through participation in peer groups and in the "school of the streets" that many black children and youth in the inner-city acquire an array of survival skills which enable them to negotiate the treacherous and sometimes life-threatening environment in which they are marooned. Such participation also prepares them for specific and often highly functional roles in the social context in which they find themselves. Role-playing, "apprenticing," and verbal contest (e.g., playing "the dozen")[60] are some of the ways in which black adolescents, through their affiliation with peer groups, develop the skills to deal with people and situations they encounter in everyday life. These behaviors also serve as a means of gaining acceptance and status among peers.[61]

For boys, the peer group is the all-important tribunal, in which identity is shaped and validated by the "brothers" on the streets. Boys are expected to be "cool" in the face of all kinds of adversity, and learn to behave accordingly. The ability to stay cool under adverse conditions is not merely a matter of style. As has been pointed out, it:

> "has a great deal to do with developing a sense of dignity and worth. Since there are so few symbols with which to augment his image—no $90,000 home, Brooks Brothers suits, or original paintings—all the man is must be conveyed in human encounters. His peers judge him accordingly: 'The cat's beautiful,' or 'He ain't shit.' Because cool is such an essential attribute and maintaining it has such an important effect on his ego, the ghetto youth would sooner go down than blow his cool, even in a situation where he has to retreat and the particular game is considered lost. The loss is not catastrophic if the brother is able to negotiate the situation and maintain control and his self-respect."[62]

In short, "being cool" involves emotional toughness, even callousness and indifference toward many of the problems and people the adolescent encounters. Through such well-organized speech events as signifying, sounding, playing the dozen, or other activities involving an exchange of insults, black males practice the art of the "cool pose" as a defense against assaults on their masculinity.

Despite the success of street-based peer groups in teaching black male adolescents the functional roles and competencies they need to survive in the social context of the inner-city, the skills so acquired are not necessarily ones which prepare these youth to function effectively in the world beyond their circumscribed environment. Indeed, since inner-city youth relate largely to their immediate environment, and much of their socialization is geared to surviving in that context, it is to be expected that they are likely to experience considerable difficulty as they venture beyond the boundaries of that world.[63] This is especially so where opportunities to assume mainstream roles are severely limited, where youth come to perceive that entering the mainstream is only a chance occurrence, and that the more realistic strategy is to perfect those skills that will enable them to exploit the opportunities their immediate environment offers for survival and self-esteem.

One of the major obvious dangers of adolescent involvement in street-based peer groups is the tendency to be drawn into the self-destructive world of crime, drugs, and violence. Since so few legitimate opportunities for employment and income are readily available to youth in the inner-city, the temptation to test their skills in the underground or street economy of the community is an attractive alternative to no job or income at all. Moreover, for youth whose failure in school impedes or denies them access to legitimate opportunities for earning an income, drug dealing, burglary, and a variety of other hustling activities may be perceived as the only means of acquiring those material possessions and lifestyles that bring prestige and approval among peers in the community.

Hence, because opportunities for developing a strong sense of identity through conventional modes of achievement are so limited, a growing number of young black males in the inner-city now find their identity in negative options. This was not always the case. For generations young black boys considered participation in sports like basketball, football, and boxing as a potential pathway to achievement, respectability, and escape from the perils of ghetto life. But, as the school dropout rate among black males in the inner-city has soared in recent decades, and as a scarcity of resources has forced many public schools to drop their athletic programs, fewer and fewer black teenagers entertain these activities as viable options, and often find in street gangs or crews the easiest pathway to identity and maturity, one requiring few skills or attributes they do not possess or cannot develop.[64]

Even so, many young black males who grow up in the inner-city seek other avenues to maturity and achievement, sometimes alternating between legitimate and deviant spheres of the mainstream and black communities. Despite hard times and almost insurmountable odds, these youth manage to retain some hope of a brighter future and are motivated to pursue their objectives. They are what have been called the "superkids," those "phenomenal youth who manage not only to survive in a community devastated by crime, drug addiction, and violence, but to be recognized as achievers and encouraged to realize their potential as fully as possible."[65] The greater proportion of these youth have benefitted from sheltering experiences established by parents, teachers, and community leaders, experiences which more or less protect them from prolonged competition on the streets by providing them with as many of the benefits of stability and education as possible, as well as opportunities to earn an income, a sense of achievement, and self-worth.[66]

Those for whom such sheltering experiences are unavailable must rely on the strength of their own resources for survival and achievement, and hope that with strong determination and a lot of luck, they will succeed in reaching their objectives. As many soon discover, however, even strong motivation and drive are frequently insufficient to neutralize or overcome the formidable obstacles to achievement and mobility they confront. As a result, cynicism and despair take hold, and chip away at endurance, leaving these young men bitter, resentful, and enraged. Some turn their anger and frustration inward on themselves, engaging in patterns of spiraling self-destructive behavior; others direct their rage toward the community, organizing themselves into roving gangs whose members terrorize the community through acts of mayhem and murder.

In short, inner-city black youth are routinely faced with moral and economic choices few are mature enough to make. Although most poor youth seek conventional opportunities to mature into competent and respected adults, their efforts frequently are stymied by the absence of constructive alternatives which engage their talents and potential, as well as their aspirations for personal achievement. Yet, even so, these youth:

"do not easily relinquish the American Dream and do not fool themselves when they take routes to maturity that are self-destructive or establish them as second-class citizens. Nor do they seek handouts, even if they take them when they are grudgingly offered in lieu of more constructive challenges. Perhaps the greatest source of frustration to adults who work with disadvantaged young people is the knowledge that every day potentially valuable minds are being wasted in hedonistic escapes because more constructive and challenging opportunities are vanishing from the communities in which they work."[67]

Thus, in the absence of a "facilitating environment" characterized by supportive adult relationships and opportunities for participating in constructive activities which strengthen ties to mainstream institutions, poor youth are free to make their own moral and economic choices in the context of spontaneous structures of socialization which are in the long term destructive to their interests and well-being. And since black boys in the inner-city are the principal participants in these male-dominated structures, they are more often the victims of their destructive influences.

CONCLUSION AND IMPLICATIONS

On the basis of a body of empirical data derived from a variety of sources, it is clear that the situation of a large and growing segment of black adolescents in the inner-cities has deteriorated significantly during the past two decades, reaching a level of crisis proportions on some indicators of social and economic well-being. This ominous development is due to a complex constellation of mutually reinforcing factors which have converged to undermine the moral and social order of the inner-city and intensify the effects of poverty and social isolation.[68]

Specifically, perverse demographic trends, deteriorating local economies, and intractable high levels of urban poverty have combined to exacerbate the problems of the inner-cities and the predicament of black adolescents. The proportion of black youths who live in central cities increased by more than 70 percent during the past two decades,[69] creating a "critical mass" of young people. It has been suggested, that, in society as in the physical world, this is the condition that can set in motion "a self-sustaining chain reaction," one that contributes to "an explosive increase in the amount of crime, addiction, and welfare dependency" in the inner-cities.[70] Under such circumstances, it is not surprising that community institutions and local labor markets have proved inadequate to meet the needs and cope with the consequences of a substantially enlarged teenage population. In addition, major declines have occurred in the supply of legitimate opportunities for black youth in education and training in central cities. Thus, problems of crime and delinquency, drug abuse, and out-of-wedlock births among black adolescents owe their existence and increase in recent decades as much to the crippling effects of poverty, inadequate education, and joblessness as to the dramatic increases in the black youth population which occurred during this period.[71]

Although poor families have almost always faced difficulties in protecting their children from the perverse influences and dangers of their neighborhoods, the magnitude and intensity of recent deterioration in the effective environment of poor black families in the inner-cities have created additional difficulties for such families in discharging their socialization responsibilities. The demise of or disharmony in the networks of supportive community institutions which functioned to facilitate the socialization of children and youth in the inner-city has exacerbated the problems poor parents, especially single parents, encounter in rearing their children. As has been suggested, not only are many of the institutions in the inner-city, including families, in disarray, and therefore "unable to provide a coordinated structure of socialization to protect the growing children and adolescents against the vicissitudes of urban living, (but) the size and complexity of such areas provide an opportunity structure for spontaneous structures of socialization to develop which are detrimental to the adolescent."[72] In fact, such spontaneous structures of socialization (i.e., gangs) have increasingly become substitutes for or extensions of the family, providing emotional, financial, and social support, as well as sources of peer-based identities which persist for some youth well into adulthood.[73]

Thus, sharp increases in economic marginality, accompanied by the progressive demise of a series of social institutions charged with the responsibility for socializing and controlling adolescents—first the family, then the school, and eventually the community—have created the conditions for the rise of alternative structures of socialization which have induced a growing number of black adolescents, particularly males, to relinquish their belief in the possibility of conventional achievement and mobility in mainstream society, and to internalize alternative values and normative orientations illegitimate in mainstream society. These trends in the attitudes and behavior of inner-city youth are every bit as important to address as are the structural or economic problems that created them. As the number of black male adolescents who come to embrace the self-destructive features associated with social disengagement from the larger society increases, the more difficult it will be to retrieve them as social and economic conditions improve.

Thus, for poor black adolescent males, no less than for females, recent structural and economic changes in the larger society and the black community have had the effect of extending the list of disadvantages many of these youth suffer most of their lives. Unlike their white male counterparts, whose experience of poverty is, on the whole, less chronic and debilitating,[74] poor black boys are exposed to a series of experiences that place them at high risk of social and psychological impairment. They are more likely to be born to unwed teenage mothers who are poorly educated and more likely to neglect or abuse their children.[75] The children of these mothers are also more likely to be born underweight and to experience injuries or neurological defects which require long-term care.[76] Moreover, such children are more likely to be labelled "slow learners" or "educable mentally retarded," to have learning difficulties in school, to lag behind their peers in basic educational competence or skills, and to drop out of school at an early age. Black boys are also more likely to be institutionalized or placed in foster care.[77] Given these cumulative disadvantages, it is remarkable that the proportion of black male adolescents who survive to become well-adjusted individuals and responsible husbands and fathers is so high, or that the percentage who drop out of school, become addicted to drugs, involved in crime, and end up in jail is not considerably greater.

As a number of studies have shown, it is not necessary to eliminate all of the risk factors to which poor children and youth are exposed in order to diminish the destructive outcomes they experience in adulthood.[78] School failure, juvenile crime, drug use and abuse, teenage pregnancy, and pregnancy outside of marriage are not the results of a single risk factor, such as being reared in an impoverished single-parent household, but are the products of multiple and interacting risk factors. Premature birth, poor health and nutrition, child abuse, family discord, and the social and economic conditions that are causal to these patterns, are all implicated in the production of damaging outcomes for black children and youth, and each multiplies the destructive effects of the others. As has been argued, "It will make a difference if we can reduce the incidence of low birth-weight or vision defects, if the isolated mother is helped to respond to her difficult infant, if more children come to school better prepared to succeed in mastering fundamental academic skills, and have reason to look forward to a better future. It will be of value if we can eliminate one risk factor or two, even if others remain."[79]

We can significantly alter the prospects for large numbers of inner-city youths by investing in and building upon programs that demonstrated success in addressing many of their needs and the needs of their families.[80] These programs, however, are quite different, in design and philosophy, from prevailing service delivery systems in that they are typically intensive, comprehensive, and flexible. That is, they provide a range of support services tailored to the unique requirements and problems of disadvantaged children and families because "they recognize that social and emotional support and concrete help (with food, housing, income, employment—or anything else that seems to the family to be an insurmountable obstacle) may have to be provided before a family can make use of other interventions, from antibiotics to advice on parenting."[81] Such intensive and comprehensive interventions are not cheap, of course, but then neither is the highly fragmented and often irrational service delivery system currently in place.

In any case, without concerted efforts to identify and implement interventions to improve the nature and quality of their experiences at home, at school, and in their neighborhoods, as well as their access to work opportunities, it is unlikely that black male adolescents in the inner-cities will be able in significant numbers to find useful roles in a society whose economic institutions are undergoing rapid change. In the absence of such efforts, many of these youth are doomed to a life of street-corner idleness, dependency, and crime. And society is doomed to bear the consequences.

NOTES

1. F.A. Ianni, *The Search for Structure: A Report on American Youth Today* (New York: The Free Press, 1989).

2. F.A. Ianni, *Home, School, and Community in Adolescent Education* (New York: Columbia University, Institute for Urban and Minority Education, 1983), 36.

3. L.J.D. Wacquant and W.J. Wilson, "The Cost of Racial and Class Exclusion in the Inner-City," *The Annals* 501 (1989): 11.

4. J.D. Kasarda, "Urban Change and Minority Opportunities," in *The New Urban Reality*, ed. P. Peterson (Washington, D.C.: Brookings Institution, 1985); and Andrew M. Sum and W. Neal Fogg, "The Adolescent Poor and the Transition to Early Adulthood," in this volume.

5. Wacquant and Wilson, "The Cost of Racial and Class Exclusion," 16.

6. R.L. Taylor, "African-American Inner-City Youth and the Subculture of Disengagement," in *Teenage Pregnancy: Developing Strategies for Change in the Twenty-First Century*, eds. D.J. Jones and S. Battle (New Brunswick, NJ: Transaction, 1990).

7. J. MacLeod, *Ain't No Makin' It: Leveled Aspirations in a Low-Income*

Neighborhood (Boulder, CO: Westview Press, 1987); T. Williams and W. Kornblum, *Growing Up Poor* (Lexington, MA: Lexington Books, 1985).

8. R.L. Taylor, "Black Youth in Crisis," *Humbolt Journal of Social Relations* 14 (1987): 106–133.

9. R.L. Taylor, "Black Youth, Role Models and the Social Construction of Identity," *Black Adolescents*, ed. R. Jones (Berkeley, CA: Cobb & Henry, 1989), chap. 8.

10. J.T. Gibbs, *Young, Black, and Male in America* (Dover, MA: Auburn House, 1988).

11. J. Ogbu, "A Cultural Ecology of Competence Among Inner-City Blacks," in *Beginnings: The Social and Affective Development of Black Children*, eds. M. Spencer, G. Brookin, and W. Allen (Hillsdale, NJ: Erlbaum, 1985).

12. Ogbu, "A Cultural Ecology," 51.

13. U. Bronfenbrenner, "Contexts of Childrearing: Problems and Prospects," *American Psychologist* 34 (1979): 844–850.

14. Ogbu, "A Cultural Ecology."

15. J. Ladner, *Tomorrow's Tomorrow: The Black Women* (New York: Doubleday, 1971); R. Clark, *Family Life and School Achievement: Why Poor Black Children Succeed or Fail* (Chicago: University of Chicago Press, 1983).

16. F. Furstenberg, R. Lincoln, and J. Mekin, *Teenage Sexuality, Pregnancy and Childbearing* (Philadelphia, PA: University of Pennsylvania Press, 1981); J. Ladner, "The Impact of Teenage Pregnancy on the Black Family: Policy Directions," in *Black Families*, ed. H. McAdoo, 2nd. ed. (Beverly Hills, CA.: Sage, 1988).

17. B. Silverstein and R. Krate, *Children of the Dark Ghetto* (New York: Praeger, 1975); V. Young, "A Black American Socialization Pattern," *American Ethnologist* 1 (1974): 515–431.

18. Ladner, *Tomorrow's Tomorrow*.

19. Silverstein and Krate, *Children*, 33.

20. Z. Blau, *Black Children/White Children: Competence, Socialization and Social Structure* (New York: Free Press, 1981). Also see D. Lewis, "The Black Family: Socialization and Sex Roles," *Phylon* 36 (1975): 221–37. According to Lewis, "age and birth order are more crucial determinants of differential treatment and behavioral expectations in black families" than sex of the child. Likewise, Schultz found no differential socialization by sex among low-income black families he studied in St. Louis. Rather, gender-specific socialization of black male adolescents occurred largely outside the home and under the tutelage of peers; see D. Schultz, *Coming Up Black: Patterns of Ghetto Socialization* (Englewood Cliffs, NJ: Prentice-Hall, 1977).

21. Blau, *Black Children/White Children*; Lewis, "The Black Family."

22. N. Hare, *Bringing the Black Boy to Manhood* (San Francisco: Black Think Tank, 1986).

23. P. Kunkel and S. Kennard, *Spout Spring: A Black Community* (New York: Holt, Rinehart and Winston, 1971); B. Hare and L.A. Castenell, "No Place to Run, No Place to Hide: Comparative Status and Future Prospects of Black Boys," in *Beginnings: The Social and Affective Development of Black Children*, eds. M. Spencer, G. Brookins, and W. Allen, (Hillsdale, NJ: Erlbaum, 1985).

24. Blau, *Black Children/White Children*, 204. Blau hypothesizes from her study of socialization practices among black and white families that the "heavy use of aversive forms of control in socializing black males, particularly, [is] a significant source of the greater proneness of black than white males to crimes of violence."

25. Hylan Lewis, "Culture, Class, and Family Life Among Low-Income Urban Negroes," in *Employment, Race, and Poverty*, eds. A. Ross and H. Hill (New York: Harcourt, Brace and World, 1967). Lewis found in his study of low-income black families in Washington, D.C. that loss of parental control, and in self-estimates of ability to control, occurs when the children are as young as five or six; see also Silverstein and Krate, *Children*; and Williams and Kornblum, *Growing Up Poor*.

26. S. Cummings, "Family Socialization and Fatalism Among Black Adolescents," *Journal of Negro Education* 46 (1977): 62–75.

27. Blau, *Black Children/White Children*; see also D. Baumrind, "Current Patterns of Parental Authority," *Developmental Psychology Monographs* 4 (1971): 1–103.

28. J. Hunt and L. Hunt, "Racial Inequality and Self-Image: Identity Maintenance as Identity Diffusion," *Sociology and Social Research* 61 (1977): 539–59; R. L. Taylor, "Black Youth, Role Models."

29. Hunt and Hunt, "Racial Inequality"; R. L. Taylor, "Black Youth, Role Models."

30. William Wilson, *The Truly Disadvantaged* (Chicago: University of Chicago Press, 1987).

31. See, for instance, L. Grant, "Black Females' 'Place' in Desegregated Classrooms," *Sociology of Education* 57 (1984): 98–111; J. Hanna, *Disruptive School Behavior: Class, Race, and Culture* (New York: Holmes & Meier, 1988); J. Irvine, *Black Students and School Failure* (New York: Greenwood Press, 1990); R.C. Rist, *The Urban School: A Factory for Failure* (Cambridge, MA: MIT Press, 1973); J. Rosenbaum, *Making Inequality: The Hidden Curriculum of High School Tracking* (New York: Wiley, 1976).

32. Carnegie Corporation of New York, "Renegotiating Society's Contract with the Public Schools," *Carnegie Quarterly* 29–30 (1984–85): 1–11.

33. For provocative analyses of how the structure of public schools affects the performance and behavior of black and other minority children, see J. Oakes, *Keeping Track: How Schools Structure Inequality* (New Haven: Yale University Press, 1985); J. Anyon, "Social Class and the Hidden Curriculum of Work," in *Curriculum and Instruction*, eds. H. Giroux, et al. (Berkeley: McCutchan, 1981); M. Apple and N. King, "What Do Schools Teach?" in, *The Hidden Curriculum and Moral Education*, eds. H. Giroux and D. Purpel (Berkeley: McCutchan, 1983).

34. Irvine, *Black Students and School Failure*.

35. J. Ogbu, "The Consequences of the American Caste System," in *The School Achievement of Minority Children*, U. Neisser, ed. (Hillsdale, NJ: Erlbaum, 1986). See also S. Fordham and J. Ogbu, "Black Students' School Success: Coping with the "Burden of 'Acting White,' " *Urban Review* 18 (1986): 176–

206; and J. Howard and R. Hammond, "Rumors of Inferiority," *The New Republic* 193 (1985): 17–21.

36. Ogbu, "The Consequences."

37. Ogbu, "The Consequences," 38.

38. A. Boykins, "The Triple Quandary and the Schooling of Afro-American Children," in Neisser, *School Achievement*; See also T. Kockman, *Black and White Styles in Conflict* (Chicago: University of Chicago Press, 1981); Hanna, *Disruptive School Behavior*; and Irvine, *Black Students*.

39. S. Hamilton, "The Social Side of Schooling: Ecological Studies of Classrooms and Schools," *Elementary School Journal* 83 (1983): 313–34.

40. Irvine, *Black Students*, p. xx.

41. See, for example, J. Brophy and T. Good, "Teachers' Communications of Differential Expectations for Children's Classroom Performance: Some Behavioral Data," *Journal of Educational Psychology* 61 (1970): 356–74; and R. Baron, D. Tom, and H. Cooper, "Social Class, Race and Teacher Expectations," *Teacher Expectancies*, J. Dusek ed. (Hillsdale, NJ: Erlbaum, 1985).

42. H. Cooper and T. Good, *Pygmalion Grows Up: Studies in the Expectation Communication Process* (New York, NY: Longman).

43. Irvine, *Black Students*.

44. Gibbs, *Young, Black, and Male*.

45. Rist, *The Urban School*.

46. Carnegie, "Renegotiating Society's Contract;" see also J. Eyler, V. Cook, and L. Ward, *Resegregation: Segregation Within Desegregated Schools*, Paper presented at the meeting of the American Education Research Association (New York, March 1982).

47. M.C. Taylor and G. Foster, "Bad Boys and School Suspension: Public Policy Implications for Black Males," *Sociological Inquiry* 56 (1986): 498–506.

48. Eyler, Cook and Ward, *Resegregation*.

49. Grant, "Black Females' 'Place' "; see also L. Grant, "Race-Gender Status, Classroom Interaction, and Children's Socialization in Elementary School," *Gender and Classroom Interaction*, L.C. Wilkerson and C.B. Marrett eds. (Orlando: Academic Press, 1985); Hare and Castenell, "No Place to Run"; R. Aaron and G. Powell, "Feedback Practices as a Function of Teacher and Pupil Race During Reading Groups Instruction," *Journal of Negro Education* 51 (1982): 50–59; A. Simpson and M. Erickson, "Teachers' Verbal and Non-Verbal Communication Patterns as a Function of Teacher Race, Student Gender, and Student Race," *American Educational Research Journal* 20 (1983): 183–98.

50. J. Irvine, "Teacher-Student Interactions: Effects of Student Race, Sex, and Grade Level," *Journal of Educational Psychology* 78 (1986): 14–21.

51. See especially J. Hunt and L. Hunt, "Racial Inequality and Self-Image" and Hare and Castenell, "No Place to Run."

52. See, for example, R. Eaves, "Teacher Race, Student Race, and Behavior Problem Checklist," *Journal of Abnormal Child Psychology* 70 (1975): 979–87; L. Grant, "Classroom Peer Relationships of Minority and Non-Minority Students," paper presented at the meeting of the American Educational

Adolescent Black Males   161

Research Association, San Francisco, CA, April 1986; Irvine, "Teacher-Student Interactions;" Irvine, *Black Students*. See also E. Smith, "The Black Female Adolescent: A Review of the Educational, Career and Psychological Literature," *Psychology of Women Quarterly* 6 (1982): 261–88. It should be noted that while the school experiences of black females tend, on the whole, to be more positive than those of their male counterparts, they encounter a somewhat different set of obstacles and different forms of negative feedback which have adverse impacts on their academic performance.

53. L. Schiamberg, "The Influence of Family on Educational and Occupational Achievement," Paper presented at the meeting of the American Association for the Advancement of Science, Philadelphia, PA, May 1986; Hare and Castenell, "No Place to Run."

54. Hare and Castenell, "No Place to Run."

55. L. Rainwater, *Behind Ghetto Walls: Black Family Life in a Federal Slum* (Chicago: Aldine, 1974); Lewis, "The Black Family."

56. Silverstein and Krate, *Children*.

57. Silverstein and Krate, *Children*, 98.

58. Silverstein and Krate, *Children*, 99.

59. E. Perkins, *Home is a Dirty Street* (Chicago: Third World Press, 1975); Ogbu, "A Cultural Ecology."

60. The "dozen," "signifying," and "sounding" refer to a game of exchanging ritualized insults that serves as a means of controlling and expressing aggression and manipulating others. For an analysis of such verbal contests, see W. Labov, *Language in the Inner City* (Philadelphia: University of Pennsylvania Press, 1972).

61. Silverstein and Krate, *Children*; Ogbu, "A Cultural Ecology."

62. D. Glasgow, *The Black Underclass* (New York: Vintage, 1981).

63. Williams and Kornblum, *Growing Up Poor*.

64. J.M. Hagedorn, *People and Folks: Gangs, Crime and The Underclass in a Rustbelt City* (Chicago: Lake View Press, 1988).

65. Williams and Kornblum, *Growing Up Poor*, 16.

66. See, for example, Clark, *Family Life*; and J. Comer, *Maggie's American Dream: The Life and Times of a Black Family* (New York: New American Library, 1988) on the role of families as shelters or buffers for youth; and Ianni, *The Search for Structure*; or Williams and Kornblum, *Growing Up Poor*, on the role of teachers and community leaders.

67. Williams and Kornblum, *Growing Up Poor*, xvi.

68. Wilson, *The Truly Disadvantaged*.

69. Taylor, "Black Youth in Crisis."

70. J.Q. Wilson, *Thinking About Crime* (New York: Basic Books, 1977), 20.

71. Taylor, "Black Youth in Crisis."

72. Ianni, *Home, School, and Community*, 71.

73. Hagedorn, *People and Folks*; MacLeod, *Ain't No Makin' It*.

74. Wilson, *The Truly Disadvantaged*.

75. Furstenberg, et al., *Teenage Sexuality*.

76. *Teenage Pregnancy: The Problem That Hasn't Gone Away*, (New York: Alan Gutmachen Institute, 1981).

77. Gibbs, *Young, Black, and Male.*

78. See especially Michael Rutter, *Changing Youth in a Changing Society: Patterns of Adolescent Development and Disorder* (Cambridge, MA: Harvard University Press, 1980); and E. Werner, *Vulnerable But Invincible: A Longitudinal Study of Resilient Children and Youth* (New York: McGraw-Hill, 1982).

79. L. Schorr, *Within Our Reach: Breaking the Cycle of Disadvantage* (New York: Doubleday, 1988), 28–29. Numerous examples of constructive interventions that can change the odds for disadvantaged children and youth are presented in this volume. For instance, the correction of a vision or hearing problem—prevalent among these children—could improve the prospects of school success for many of these children by eliminating these preventable disabilities. Indeed, since early health problems appear to be a significant factor contributing to later antisocial activities, taking such corrective actions would have benefits far beyond the school experience. See, for example, C. Murray, *The Link Between Learning Disabilities and Juvenile Delinquency: Current Theory and Knowledge*, Washington, D.C.: National Institute for Juvenile Justice and Delinquency Prevention (1976); and, Rutter, *Changing Youth.*

80. A survey and description of many of these successful programs across the country is presented in Schorr, *Within Our Reach.* For a discussion of successful training and employment programs for disadvantaged youth, see R. Taylor, "Improving the Status of Black Youth: Some Lessons From Recent National Experiments," *Youth and Society* 22 (1990): 85–107.

81. Schorr, *Within Our Reach*, 256–257.

ABOUT THE AUTHORS

ROBERT COLES is a research psychiatrist for the Harvard University Health Services, as well as Professor of Psychiatry and Medical Humanities at the Harvard Medical School. He received his A.B. from Harvard University and M.D. from Columbia University College of Physicians and Surgeons. He is co-founder and member of the Board of Directors of the Center for Documentary Studies at Duke University. He is the author of numerous articles and books. The most recent is *The Spiritual Life of Children.*

PETER B. EDELMAN is associate dean and Professor of Law at Georgetown University Law Center. He received his J.D. from Harvard Law School. He was director of the New York State Division for Youth, Vice President of the University of Massachusetts, served as Legislative Assistant to Senator Robert F. Kennedy, and clerk to Supreme Court Justice Arthur J. Goldberg. He is the author of several articles on poverty, welfare and youth issues.

JOYCE A. LADNER is Vice President for Academic Affairs and Professor of Social Work at Howard University. She received her M.A. and Ph.D. in sociology from Washington University. She has taught at the Graduate School and University Center, City University of New York and Hunter College, City University of New York. She has conducted extensive research projects, and is the author of several books, articles and op-ed pieces. Her most recent article is "Debunking the Myth of the Underclass," *The Presidential Series of the American Sociological Association,* published in 1990.

JUDITH S. MUSICK is on the research faculty at the Erikson Institute for Advanced Study in Child Development. She has been a Visiting Scholar at Northwestern University and is Vice-Chair for the Ounce of Prevention Fund. She received her B.A. from Mundelein College and Ph.D. in Child Development from Northwestern University. She was director of the Thresholds Mothers' Project of the NIMH Research and Demonstration Program and has taught at the Institute for Psychoanalysis. She is the author of several articles and books. She has served on numerous boards and advisory panels.

LAURENCE STEINBERG is Professor of Psychology at Temple University, where he is also Senior Research Associate at the Center for Research in Human Development and Education. He received his Ph.D. from Cornell University. He also has taught at the University of California-Irvine and the University of Wisconsin-Madison. He is the author of several books and articles, including *You and Your Adolescent: A Parent's Guide for Ages 10 to 20*.

ANDREW M. SUM is Professor of Economics and Director of the Center for Labor Market Studies at Northeastern University. W. NEAL FOGG is a research associate at the Center for Labor Market Studies. The two authors have collaborated on a series of recent research studies on the employment and earnings experiences of young adults, the labor market for older workers and the economic and social well-being of the nation's young families. Their recent research on these topics has appeared in *Turbulence in the American Workplace, Toward a More Perfect Union* and *Vanishing Dreams: The Growing Economic Plight of America's Young Families*.

RONALD L. TAYLOR is Professor and former chair in the Department of Sociology at the University of Connecticut-Storrs. He received his Ph.D. from Boston University. He has authored and edited numerous articles and books. His most recent article was "Improving the Status of Black Youth: Some Lessons From Recent National Experiments," in *Youth and Society*, published in 1990.